Building Online Stores with osCommerce: Beginner Edition

Step by step introduction to osCommerce

David Mercer

PUBLISHING

BIRMINGHAM - MUMBAI

Building Online Stores with osCommerce: Beginner Edition

Step by step introduction to osCommerce

First published: January 2006

Published by Packt Publishing Ltd.
32 Lincoln Road
Olton
Birmingham, B27 6PA, UK.

ISBN 1-904811-88-4

www.packtpub.com

Cover Design by www.visionwt.com

Credits

Author
David Mercer

Reviewers
Monika Mathé
Theodore S. Boomer

Technical Editor
Niranjan Jahagirdar
Nanda Padmanabhan
Abhishek Shirodkar

Editorial Manager
Dipali Chittar

Development Editor
Louay Fatoohi

Indexer
Niranjan Jahagirdar

Proofreader
Chris Smith

Production Coordinator
Manjiri Nadkarni

Cover Designer
Helen Wood

About the Author

David Mercer was born in August 1976 in Harare, Zimbabwe. Having always had a strong interest in science, David came into regular contact with computers at university where he minored in Computer Science.

As a programmer and professional writer, he has written both code and books for about seven years. He has worked on a number of well-known titles, in various capacities, on a wide variety of topics. This has afforded him a singularily unique oversight into the world of programming and technology as it relates to furthering the goals of business.

David finds that the challenges arising from the dichotomous relationship between the science (and art) of software programming and the art (and science) of writing is what keeps his interest in producing books piqued. He intends to continue to write professionally in the future.

As a consultant for his own technical and editorial consultancy, David balances his time between programming, reviewing, writing, and furthering his studies in Applied Mathematics. When he isn't working (which isn't that often), he enjoys playing guitar and getting involved in outdoor activities ranging from touch rugby and golf to water skiing and snowboarding.

You can contact him at `davidm@contechst.com`, or alternatively, visit his consultancy's website at `http://www.contechst.com/`.

A big thanks to the team at Packt Publishing for giving me the opportunity to work on this book. I also thank my family and friends as well as my girlfriend, Bronagh. They have all done a great job of supporting and encouraging me over the last six months or so.
Ad astra per aspera.

About the Reviewers

Monika Mathé fascinated by anything combining logic and creativity, it seems that destiny found me in 1999 when I became a software developer and Oracle-certified database administrator.

It was a tough call to decide in which field to work, but landing a position in a marketing agency and working with everything from Oracle to SQL Server and HTML, ASP, and JavaScript was a fabulous decision I still congratulate myself for! I learned more about marketing campaigns, e-commerce, and CRMs than I had ever wanted to know, I mean, ever thought was possible!

I have also been taken in by the open-source community; I've become an avid believer in PHP (perhaps a bit less in MySQL), and definitely in a love affair with osCommerce. I believe almost anything can be done with it ... I challenge anyone to prove me wrong!

I am an active member of the osCommerce online community and know preemptively which questions will arise in new shop creation. Presently, I am creating as many new shops for customers as time allows, of course, while urging them to add as many custom coded modules as I see fit ... that's dessert for me!

Theodore S. Boomer while recovering from an extended illness, I was on my computer searching for something to challenge my mind. I found HTML. At first it was very basic, but quickly it grew as competing browsers and then HTML editors progressed. I have supplemented my knowledge with additional learning through online communities, groups, some colleges, and books from Pack-IT, which have enabled me to keep an edge on software that I can incorporate to give me a competitive edge in design.

Now I have taken the many hours I have spent finding sources to complete client projects and consolidated them into my web design business and expanded to an Internet Business Technologies company that provides web development, web hosting, systems development, merchant card services, and high-speed Internet connections from entrepreneurs to Fortune 50 companies.

Table of Contents

Introduction

The modern day entrepreneur, or indeed a business of any kind, small or large, can scarcely do without some form of presence on the Web. The pervasiveness of the Internet has brought about a new reality for business people. No longer is it sufficient to set up shop somewhere and sit quietly waiting for customers. Instead, the initiative must be taken with goods and services being marketed and sold online, reaching hitherto unheard of sizes of consumer markets, nationally and internationally.

With the added burden of the acquisition of IT skills, many small to medium-size enterprises have found themselves being outstripped by their larger cousins, who have the resources and manpower to harness and utilize the Internet properly. Prohibitively expensive development costs or ill-fitting off-the-shelf applications have hampered SME's ability to compete on an even footing. Up until now that is!

With the advent of osCommerce and other open-source technologies like it, the door has been opened for anyone with a bit of determination to set up a sophisticated online store that will hold its own against any other site out there. It's not surprising that osCommerce is growing in popularity as more and more people switch to the advantages of building and running their very own e-commerce website.

Unfortunately, while running and administering your own site is now within your grasp, you will find that you still have to work at it. There is a lot of information you need to learn about installing, configuring, customizing, securing and running osCommerce, and indeed the technologies you will be basing your business on. You can also benefit from some general wisdom and knowledge that programmers apply to their everyday work. Providing you with this knowledge is why I have written this book!

What This Book Covers

Chapter 1 introduces us to e-commerce and osCommerce and then provides an overview of the osCommerce community. Knowing how to use this excellent resource ensures you take full advantage of the entire osCommerce package, and not just the free software.

Chapter 2 covers setup and installation topics, which includes a discussion on what you should look for in an Internet servcice provider and how to make use of FTP to upload files, amongst other things. A troubleshooting section is also included and once this chapter is finished you should have a working osCommerce site up and running.

Chapter 3 deals with the most common configuration settings that you will need to familiarize yourself with and provides a basic grounding in the use of the administration tool.

Chapter 4 gets right to the heart of the matter with an in-depth look at data in osCommerce. Here you will learn not only how to add and remove products and manufacturers as well as administer orders and customers, but also how to properly design your category/product hierarchy.

Chapter 5 is where the standard look and feel of osCommerce gets a face-lift. After reading this, you will have a sound knowledge of the presentation related features of osCommerce. Additionally, we will discuss the all important topics of stylesheet modification, images, and language and show how to deal with them effectively. Get ready to get your hands dirty as there is plenty of work in here.

Chapter 6 takes you one step closer to running an online business by comprehensively dealing with taxes, payments, and shipping. Strategies for implementing various policies pertaining to money matters are also scrutinized and by the end of this chapter, you will be well versed in your site's money matters.

Chapter 7 is arguably the most important of all. The integrity of your e-commerce site (and for many of you, your livelihood) rests on how well you can implement security and disaster recovery policies. Follow along here to learn how to gain a peaceful night's sleep, safe in the knowledge that your precious business is safe. It also introduces you to some important tools, which will no doubt make your life a lot easier in the time to come. As well as this, it takes a more lighthearted look at some neat tricks and how to make a few nice touch additions.

Appendix A provides you with a look at various methods, which can be used to effectively deal with problems and errors. Having a programmer's perspective and embracing a sound methodology will save you countless hours and frustration and is applicable to a wide range of software, not just osCommerce.

Conventions

In this book, you will find a number of styles of text that distinguish between different kinds of information. Here are some examples of these styles and an explanation of their meaning.

There are three styles for code. Code words in text are shown as follows: "We can include other contexts through the use of the `include` directive."

A block of code will be set as follows:

```
if (substr(basename($PHP_SELF), 0, 8) != 'checkout') {
    include(DIR_WS_BOXES . 'languages.php');
    include(DIR_WS_BOXES . 'currencies.php');
}
```

When we wish to draw your attention to a particular part of a code block, the relevant lines or items will be made bold:

```
[if (substr(basename($PHP_SELF), 0, 8) != 'checkout') {
    // include(DIR_WS_BOXES . 'languages.php');
    include(DIR_WS_BOXES . 'currencies.php');
}
```

Any command-line input and output is written as follows:

```
mysql> insert into user values (
    -> 'localhost',
    -> 'oscommerce',
    -> Password('password'),
    -> 'Y','Y', 'Y', 'Y', 'Y','Y', 'Y'
    -> 'N','N', 'N','N', 'N','N', 'N','N', 'N','N', 'N',
    -> 'N','N', 'N','N', 'N','N', 'N','N', 'N','N');
```

New terms and **important words** are introduced in a bold-type font. Words that you see on the screen, in menus or dialog boxes for example, appear in our text like this: "clicking the Next button moves you to the next screen".

Tips, suggestions, or important notes appear in a box like this.

Reader Feedback

Feedback from our readers is always welcome. Let us know what you think about this book, what you liked or may have disliked. Reader feedback is important for us to develop titles that you really get the most out of.

To send us general feedback, simply drop an email to feedback@packtpub.com, making sure to mention the book title in the subject of your message.

If there is a book that you need and would like to see us publish, please send us a note in the SUGGEST A TITLE form on http://www.packtpub.com or email suggest@packtpub.com.

If there is a topic that you have expertise in and you are interested in either writing or contributing to a book, see our author guide on www.packtpub.com/authors.

Customer Support

Now that you are the proud owner of a Packt book, we have a number of things to help you to get the most from your purchase.

Errata

Although we have taken every care to ensure the accuracy of our contents, mistakes do happen. If you find a mistake in one of our books—maybe a mistake in text or code—we would be grateful if you would report this to us. By doing this you can save other readers from frustration, and help to improve subsequent versions of this book. If you find any errata, report them by visiting http://www.packtpub.com/support, selecting your book, clicking on the Submit Errata link, and entering the details of your errata. Once your errata have been verified, your submission will be accepted and the errata added to the list of existing errata. The existing errata can be viewed by selecting your title from http://www.packtpub.com/support.

Questions

You can contact us at questions@packtpub.com if you are having a problem with some aspect of the book, and we will do our best to address it.

1

Introduction to E-Commerce with osCommerce

When Tim Berners-Lee first decided it would be a good idea if his computer could exchange information with his colleagues' computers up the corridor, he could scarcely have known that he was setting in motion, perhaps, the most profound change in the way mankind communicates since the written word. With the advent of the **World Wide Web (WWW)**, communication underwent a kind of revolution that had an impact on our daily lives in hundreds of different ways.

Of course, it also wasn't long before someone figured out how to make money from the Web and naturally everyone jumped on the bandwagon. Enter the dotcom boom and bust! Unfortunately, for the Internet and consequently Internet-based businesses, the dotcom fiasco hurt a lot of people who perhaps, buoyed up by bullish sentiment from investment houses and brokers who understood all too well the amount of money they stood to make, invested in something they didn't fully understand. At the time, very few Internet-based businesses had shown that they were reliable, stable, and profitable. Nevertheless, the money kept flowing in and the new technology companies kept spending it—on what, no one was quite sure.

However, when the bubble burst, not all Internet initiatives collapsed. Some came through it a little worse for wear, but far more resilient, and many more learned valuable lessons about how to approach this new platform for commerce and trade. It is a testament to the exceptional value of the WWW that despite the massive losses made initially on this technology, it is now more or less taken for granted that businesses of any size require a presence on the Web: if they don't have one yet, they are going to have one soon.

Today the world recognizes that being able to retail online to potentially billions of customers on a global scale is not the panacea it was first touted to be. Instead, a more mature approach needs to be adopted. It is now the accepted viewpoint that while having the ability to interact on the Web is a critical tool for success in today's world, it is still just that—a tool! In order to be successful, your business still needs to be based on a solid idea, with a good demand or client base, backed up by either great products or great services. Just like the good old days.

By purchasing this book, you have implicitly given a vote of confidence to the Web and will, hopefully, be able to turn it to your advantage. Before we are able to begin working directly on the site, it is imperative that you are equipped with some basic information about life and business on the Internet.

This chapter discusses the following topics:

- A brief history and motivation for osCommerce and e-commerce
- The osCommerce community in general

Before we continue, it is important to realize that as things stand, our global village is still undergoing a revolution in communication driven by the giant leaps in the sophistication of both hardware and software alike. While it seems that everything is becoming more advanced and therefore complicated, the one thing to remember is that pretty much everything you see around us is here to make things easier. One of the best things about advances in technology is that they give everyone the ability to leapfrog stages of development. What this means is that the companies that invest a lot of money in order to be innovative and stay ahead of the competition blaze a trail that is decidedly easier for those of us without unlimited funding to follow.

A good example of leapfrogging is happening with technology in Africa. In many countries, poor infrastructure hampers business and communication. Luckily for them, laying hundreds of thousands of kilometers of phone line is no longer necessary, as it was for countries in the West seventy years ago. Nowadays, telecommunications companies install their own towers and the public has instant access to cellular or wireless communications. In ten short years, some African states have gone from utilizing ageing, outdated copper wire systems to modern cellular communications without having to invest their resources in research and development.

This idea applies very much to software application development and in the same way, we are going to piggy-back a ride on the work of others (in this case, the osCommerce development team) to arrive at a sophisticated and functional e-commerce website without having to re-invent the wheel. This is good news for everyone concerned, because it means that one no longer has to have a PhD in computer science in order to build and operate a fairly complex Internet-based software application.

For a lot of us, the urge to dive straight into the building of the site is all but overwhelming because, after all, that is where the magic happens. Don't do it! Instead, take a deep breath, grab a cup of coffee and read through this chapter before doing anything else. While it may seem like a drag now, it will save you a lot of time, frustration, and sanity later.

What is E-Commerce?

Before we dive into anything specific to osCommerce, let's take a closer look at what the term **e-commerce** means, just to ensure we are all reading off the same page.

> We define e-commerce as commercial transactions occurring over computer networks, facilitated by electronic applications.

Granted, this definition is pretty vague, but given the huge number of different businesses interacting over a variety of platforms and technologies all over the globe, it serves as a good basis for our purpose. In this instance, 'commercial transactions' can be taken to mean anything from buying and selling to marketing and distributing; 'electronic applications' means, in this instance, your osCommerce website.

Remember that it is crucially important that you plan ahead, and decide exactly what you require from your online store before you go ahead and begin building it. E-commerce applications are, by necessity, fairly complex beasts (even when most of the hard work has been done for us by osCommerce), and taking the time to learn about what you want from your application is time well spent.

Is there anything else we can say about e-commerce? Well, while there are many similarities between conventional and virtual enterprises since both have fundamentally the same goals, the differences can be devastating. Let's say, for example, you have set up a conventional business, for argument's sake, a bakery, and after one week you find that the new oven is not powerful enough to bake your bread quickly. As upsetting as it may be, you will probably have to go and buy another one. And while that problem has a painful solution, it is at least obvious.

This is where a conventional enterprise and a computer-based enterprise can vary greatly because, if instead of an incorrect oven specification, the virtual enterprise application accidentally utilized differing parameters (say, units of measurement) in some of its code, then it is entirely possible you could lose a $125 million Mars exploration vehicle just like NASA did in the late nineties. The loss of the Mars orbiter has, hopefully, highlighted areas where NASA's processes need to be looked at again, but the point of this is that the fault was not immediately obvious until it was too late. For those of us without a few hundred million dollars in lessons to be learned, a little planning should help ensure our more modest efforts don't suffer the same fate.

This brief section has highlighted what we mean by e-commerce and compared it with conventional commerce. However, the book is not intended to give you an in-depth discussion about best practices when it comes to planning your application. It is rather intended to help you achieve the most common and important tasks associated with running a conventional osCommerce Website. Of course, just because this book doesn't discuss planning issues doesn't exempt you from jotting down your requirements or researching your site.

Let's continue…

The What and Why of osCommerce

osCommerce has been around since March 2000 and was originally founded by Harald Ponce de Leon. The development of osCommerce is still overseen by Harald, but has also since become the domain of a full team of dedicated people. You can read about the osCommerce team on the `http://www.oscommerce.com/about/team` page. At present there are about 6,000 live, registered osCommerce sites and about 70,000 registered community members. With the rising success and popularity of this remarkable piece of software, these numbers are all set to increase dramatically.

Looking at how long osCommerce has been around, it's safe to say that there has been enough time for the technology to mature and for people to be confident that it has endured plenty of use and has been reworked and debugged to the point where it is stable and reliable. If you are not someone who is readily convinced, a visit to the osCommerce community forums at http://forums.oscommerce.com/ will demonstrate that there is a lively, active community supporting this technology—proof enough that osCommerce is working for others, and that there is the interest to push osCommerce forward in the years to come.

Quite apart from all this, it is fair enough and important to ask "*Why should I use osCommerce?*" at this early stage. Part of the answer to this seemingly innocuous question goes straight to the heart of an issue that has led to a massive divergence in one of the fundamental socio-economic questions surrounding modern computing.

There are two schools of thought that divide most programmers and developers firmly into two camps, which compete against each other, in some cases, quite vehemently. The issue is whether or not intellectual property (in particular, software) should be made available for everyone in the world to use, modify, and contribute to, or whether it should be protected.

It is strongly urged that you avail yourself of the facts when it comes to open source technology, if for nothing else than that it allows you to form a considered opinion about the software upon which your business relies. The following is a fairly good definition of the term **Open Source**:

> Open Source is defined as any program whose source code is made available—most often subject to certain conditions—for use or modification by users or other developers as they deem fit.

Open source software is usually developed as a public collaboration and is freely available. For more information on what open source is, check out http://www.opensource.org/.

So, we know that osCommerce is an open source initiative—big deal! How does this change anything or how should it influence our decision to use it? Well, let's look at some of the advantages of the open source paradigm and relate it to what you can expect from the overall osCommerce experience:

- **Totally free**: It might cost you tens or hundreds of thousands of dollars to get a software development company to build you a fully functional commercial site from scratch. Not having to pay for this development removes one of the largest obstacles that retards e-commerce growth for the small to medium enterprise.

- **Secure and stable milestone releases**: The osCommerce core has become a secure and stable environment for online commerce due of the large amount of community participation. This doesn't mean it is impervious to attack—like any other software, it has weaknesses—but you can be sure of a swift community response to any new threats that may appear.

- **Large development community**: osCommerce's source code is readily available and free to modify and so there are thousands of developers who test and improve it on a daily basis. osCommerce effectively has an unlimited development team, and with the software gaining in popularity, new code will be produced at a faster rate.

- **Large support community**: osCommerce has a large support community. This is due to the fact that the open source paradigm encourages the development of communities that feel a collective responsibility to aid others within that community.

While the above points might not seem like a big thing now, knowing that there is someone else who has perhaps struggled with the same issues that you have, and is willing to spend time to help you solve your own problems is a huge benefit that can't really be quantified in terms of cost.

Apart from the previously listed advantages that have been automatically bestowed upon osCommerce users, it is also fair to say that this is one of the world's truly valuable pieces of software that is leveling the playing ground between enterprises with large pockets and those with tighter budgets. This is because it empowers people to act on their ideas and bring their services and products to the world, via the medium of the World Wide Web, without being subject to high development costs. Removing obstacles in doing business stimulates growth and helps everyone in the long run. Hopefully, you will embrace the spirit of open source and encourage others to join in the future.

The osCommerce Online Community

Having a good technical know-how is one thing, but being able to effectively use the osCommerce community is at times equally important. Part of learning how to use osCommerce effectively must, at some point, take into account that no one needs to develop applications in isolation. The opportunity to learn from other peoples' mistakes before you fall into the same traps is a great boon for budding website developers. Even better, once you have encountered a problem, it is a pretty safe bet that someone else probably has had that same problem and already dealt with it, which means that a solution might be available on the forums.

Apart from providing ready-made solutions to problems, as well as a huge repository of information, the osCommerce community is a *living* entity with which we can all interact. Exchanging ideas and information is an integral part of learning and the open source ethos suits the learning-as-a-collective paradigm very well. Just as important is the Contributions section, which can provide you with hundreds of different add-ons to do almost anything you can conceive of without having to write the code yourself. Consequently, it is imperative that you know how to manage and use this valuable resource.

Contributions

One of the great things about programming is the ability to reuse code. This means that if some PHP guru decides he or she needs to extend the functionality provided by default with osCommerce, they can write the code that will perform the task they have in mind, and can then make that code available to everyone. Sounds almost too good to be true, but this *is* in fact true, and you can browse through the contributions section at http://www.oscommerce.com/community/contributions/ to take a look for yourself.

This resource provides a categorized list of all the different contributions available to users like you and me. All the contributions listed on the site are provided freely under the GNU general public license (make sure you read and understand any additional license information provided with a contribution). It's worth checking this out, and you can find a copy of the license at `http://www.gnu.org/copyleft/gpl.html`. Other than providing a categorized list of contributions, there are also two options to search through the latest and most downloaded packages.

It is important to realize that these contributions are often developed by individuals, and while they are an excellent resource, at times they can contain bugs. You will notice that many of the download pages have multiple versions of each package—each one fixing bugs or improving on the last version. Accordingly, you should always approach the use of contributions with caution, and at all times endeavor to understand exactly how the package is working to achieve its tasks.

Once we start adding some advanced functionality, we will come back to this topic and run through how to download, install, and modify community contributions.

Forums

The idea behind the **osCommerce Forums** is to provide a kind of huge noticeboard for everyone involved in osCommerce to ask questions and search for answers. It also provides a convenient way to meet other people in the same boat, which can be a useful means of sharing ideas and discussing technical issues with people at the same level of experience. Specifically, the following interesting and useful topics, among others, can be found at the osCommerce forums:

- News and announcements
- General support
- Installation and configuration
- Tips and tricks
- Contribution announcements
- Contribution support
- General chitchat
- Next steps
- E-commerce laws

With approximately 70,000 registered users and hundreds of people online at any given time, it is certain that you will find at least a part of the answer you need from the forums. However, bear in mind that like any public service, there are rules and guidelines to abide by when using these facilities. A quick read over the rules at `http://forums.oscommerce.com/index.php?act=boardrules` should avoid any infringements of netiquette.

One of the main points to remember is that you should make an honest effort to search for similar posts before adding your own post to any of the lists—obviously it is nice to keep redundancy in the lists to a minimum. This is quite a big point because it is notoriously hard to find the exact postings you are looking for. The forum gives you the option of ordering the posts based on a few criteria, searching for only those posts posted recently, and so on.

Of course, you are encouraged to register as a forum user in order to make use of the forums properly—you will find that you are able to use the search features without any problems.

Knowledge Base

The **osCommerce Knowledge Base** takes a different approach to help osCommerce users. It is more of a documentation effort taking the form of a series of articles that describe a wide variety of osCommerce issues and topics. Navigating to the homepage for the knowledge base at `http://www.oscommerce.info/` gives the following page:

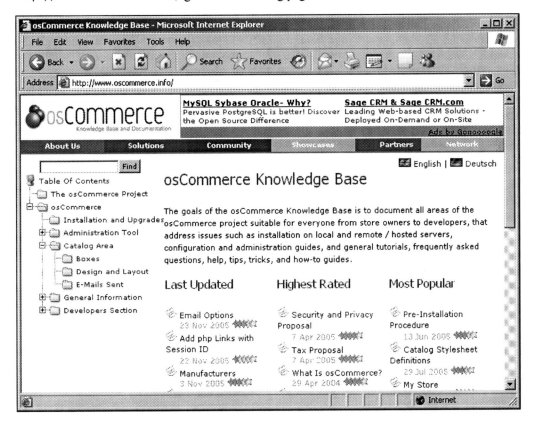

As you can see, the list on the left-hand side provides a categorized table of articles, which is really easy to use. Each article covers a single topic, and all of them can be ranked in terms of how useful you found them. The downside is that not everything has had an article written about it yet. So, while this may be the answer for your more run-of-the-mill queries, it is unlikely that it will provide you with a solution or example for more complex problems. Having said this, it is a community project, and new articles are added all the time—definitely something worth using and supporting.

Documentation

The official documentation is available online *and* as a download. It is recommended that you use the downloadable version, since this will be available to you whenever you need it regardless of whether an Internet connection is available. The documentation uses a different method from the forums and knowledge base. This time, each aspect of osCommerce is briefly discussed in an easy-to-navigate HTML-based hierarchy. A complete listing can be found in the table of contents at `http://www.oscommerce.info/docs/english/table_of_contents.html`. Perusing this is definitely worthwhile for novice and experienced osCommerce users alike, although many of you will find the information a bit terse or even sparse in places.

Bug and Progress Reports

Another worthwhile exercise is to look at the bug reports at `http://www.oscommerce.com/community/bugs/`, which are nicely categorized, and are assigned to various experienced members of the community to either verify and act upon or dismiss as bogus. At the very least, browsing the bug lists provides a good method of seeing whether any problems you may have been experiencing could be the result of a *bug*. If you do suspect a *bug* in your installation of osCommerce, you should report it, but only after you have made certain it is not simply inexplicable behavior. Obviously, every bug report needs to be looked at, so it consumes someone's time and effort to investigate a report—make reports only after some deliberation.

Progress reports can be found at `http://www.oscommerce.com/community/reports` and are very useful in terms of keeping abreast of the latest news within the osCommerce community. For example, the latest update at the time of writing (`http://www.oscommerce.com/community/reports,115`) contained information on the following and more:

- **Team Reorganization**: The osCommerce team has been reorganized to optimize the amount of resources available, and to spread responsibilities throughout the team.

- **New Support Site Navigation Menu**: A new navigation menu has been added to the support site, which now offers drop-down menu entries to the pages in each section of the support site.

- **Forum Structure Updates**: The forum structure has been updated to improve the usability of which postings should be made in which forum channels.

- **Daylight Saving Time On The Forum**: To correctly set the time on the forums to reflect daylight saving time, please go to your Control Panel | Options | Board Settings and select the "Is daylight saving time in effect?" option.

- **Knowledge Base Update**: A Table of Contents has been added to the knowledge base site to provide an overview of all knowledge base articles currently available.

- **Most Downloaded Contributions**: The Contributions section has been updated to allow browsing the contribution packages ordered by the most downloaded.

Obviously, this is all pretty pertinent information for the active osCommerce community member. Talking of being an active community member, a pretty fair statement about the community, of which you are now a member, is that you get out what you put in. The online community is a great resource, and with your help it will only improve.

Summary

Hopefully, at this stage, you have practiced using the osCommerce community, registered on the site, and learned a bit about the forums. Being able to use this resource efficiently will be a great help in the time to come. Consequently, this chapter focused predominantly on what is available from the osCommerce community and how you can make use of it to find news, learn about new developments, or share and discuss ideas and problems.

It is a well known fact that many new users run into a couple of problems and end up becoming disillusioned with their e-commerce software (this applies to all e-commerce software and not just osCommerce), dismissing it as difficult to use. The unfortunate thing here is that often their problems are readily solved and it is their lack of ability to use the significant osCommerce resources to do so that is their undoing.

It's not all doom and gloom! At least 70,000 people are happily chugging along with their online osCommerce stores, and with a little help you will be joining them shortly. So, for better or for worse, you have decided to join the fray and from here on, you will find new things to learn and put to work for you and your business. Let's get cracking...

2

Setting Up osCommerce

Now that you can rest easy, safe in the knowledge that you are backed by an entire community's worth of information and resources, it is time to try out osCommerce for real. Most likely, this section should present little to no difficulty whatsoever because osCommerce now comes as part and parcel of many hosting packages. If you haven't already purchased a hosting package then you might want to ask around in order to find one that supports osCommerce by default.

Of course, I would be remiss if I didn't cover how to set everything up properly from start to finish and, to this end, this chapter will cover the following topics:

- Your Site's Basic Requirements
- Downloading osCommerce
- Transferring osCommerce to your Live Site
- Making sure the host is ready
- Installing and configuring osCommerce
- Troubleshooting

That's a fair amount of material to cover but you should not feel overwhelmed by this because it is generally in a software producer's best interest to make it as easy as possible for their clients to download and install software. If they don't then they leave a gap for someone else to improve on their process. Because the best way to make things easy to understand is by providing a logical and consistent approach to obtaining and installing their software, you will find that for more or less anything you want to get hold of (in this case osCommerce), there is a fairly straightforward and simple process.

Another point to mention is that in order to demonstrate many of the concepts and tasks which will be needed for you to set up your own store, this book will build up a fictional enterprise called Contechst Books, which can be viewed at `http://www.contechst.com/catalog/`. By demonstrating changes on a real live store, you will be better equipped to relate the changes made to your site's configuration, customization, and administration to what the customer sees and how he or she uses your store.

No doubt you will be up and running in no time, but if you do experience any problems, please see the troubleshooting section presented at the end of this chapter. Hopefully it will be able to guide you to a solution even if it can't present the exact one straight away. With that said, let's begin…

Your Site's Basic Requirements

The first thing you need is a web domain, which will allow people to visit your site by typing in your business's **URI (Universal Resource Indicator)**. There are plenty of excellent hosting packages available online, and you should choose one based on the criteria that suit your business's needs the best. Ensuring that you understand what your site is likely to need in the future is a good way to determine what type of hosting package you need now.

You might want to think about ensuring you have FTP capability for transferring files to the host—this is not entirely necessary, so wait until you have read the section entitled *Transferring osCommerce to Your Live Site* a little later on in this chapter. More often than not, you should be able to log on to your FTP account with your administrator's username and password automatically. If you're not sure what all this is about, then try the following URL in your browser (assuming your browser supports FTP): `ftp://ftp.your_domain_name.com`

If you are prompted for a password or are shown the contents of your home directory, then congratulations, you have an FTP account. If you don't have one, then you should consider getting your host to give you one, or finding out from them how they upload files. Incidentally, instead of being prompted for your username and password every time you use your FTP account, you might want to send them in the URL, like so: `ftp://username:password@hostname/`

If you're worried about security (by this I mean: you *are* worried about security), then it's best to leave out the password and simply pass the username, because this can cause security problems if URLs are logged in a non-secure place.

A quick recap of the bare necessities you require from a hosting package is as follows:

- **Apache:** Used to serve web pages. Your host will need to make use of Apache as its web server of choice as opposed to something like Microsoft's IIS.

- **PHP:** Your host must provide support for PHP since this is the language in which osCommerce is written.

- **MySQL:** You should also be able to obtain a MySQL account for use by osCommerce since this is what drives the data, or back end, of the osCommerce application.

You might also want to make sure the provider is giving you enough hard disk space to safely run the business. Remember that you will probably have a lot of log files and a fair number of images as well as data in your database. They should also provide some form of SSL support, depending on what your security needs will be. Beyond that, you should also look for fair pricing, reliability (specifically, look for percentage downtime), and ease of use, as well as email facilities.

Since many hosts have the three pieces of software installed by default, as part of their hosting package, it is quite likely that they also come with the option to simply enable osCommerce on your domain. It is obviously very easy to install osCommerce on your live site this way (generally it is simply a case of clicking on the osCommerce option and supplying a username and password for your administrative duties) and you should simply follow any instructions given by your hosts or contact their support if you have any queries.

If, however, your hosting plan does not come with the option to enable osCommerce by default then you will need to download a copy and ensure it gets to your live site in one piece.

Downloading osCommerce

Without further ado, we are going to head off to the osCommerce site and grab a copy for ourselves at http://www.oscommerce.com/solutions/downloads. At the time of writing, the current milestone is 2.2 and this is the version you should use unless the next milestone has come out in the interim. Which version you use won't make a huge difference with respect to the material in this book.

> It is strongly recommended that you also download the documentation from this page, since you will find it full of invaluable advice, hints, and tips.

Choose whether you would like to download osCommerce from Europe or the States by clicking on the relevant link, and save the download to your My Documents folder (or wherever you find most suitable). Notice that the download itself is only about 1.4 MB, so it's unlikely that you will have time to go and have that all-important cup of coffee while you wait—unless you are on a particularly slow dial-up connection.

Once the file has downloaded, extract it to the same folder. You will find that everything is contained within a directory called something like oscommerce-2.2ms2 depending on which version you are using. If you open up this main directory, you will see that it contains a folder called catalog. Zip up this folder, and call the new file catalog.zip. Once that is done you are ready to transfer the catalog folder over to the host.

Transferring osCommerce to Your Live Site

It should be mentioned at this point that if you are thinking of doing a fair amount of work on the default site, then you are advised to actually work on a *copy* of the site on your own PC. This entails setting up what is a called a **Development Environment** on your machine; the idea being that you do all the hard work offline and only deploy the finished product to your live site.

However, this means that you have to install PHP, Apache, and MySQL before you install osCommerce and ensure that they are all up and running and working together before you can do any work at all. Since the aim of this book is to teach you specifically about osCommerce we do not cover any of that here. For more information on how to set up a development environment, you can take a look at the professional edition of this book, *Building Online Stores with osCommerce: Professional Edition* (ISBN 1-904811-14-0), or simply do a search on Google for installation instructions and work from there.

By far the easiest method would be to use a native upload feature from your host's file manager over a quick connection. If this is available to you, simply use it to upload the archive file across to the host server. The following screenshot shows how this is achieved using the demo site's host:

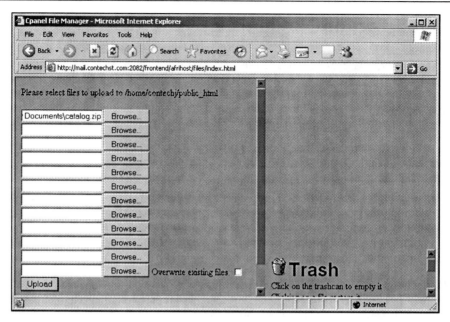

Alternatively, assuming your site has an FTP account enabled, the following two methods represent a quick and painless method of uploading files with FTP.

FTP Drag and Drop

Windows users can open up the host file system using an FTP account in Windows Explorer or Internet Explorer and simply drag the catalog .zip folder from their file systems over to the host site, as shown here:

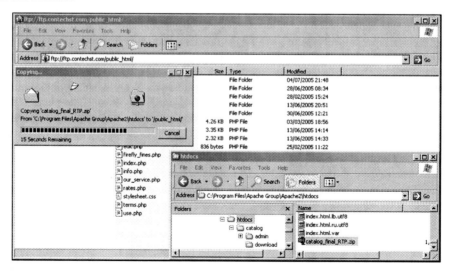

There are a few things to note about the previous screenshot. First, even though you can't see it, I had to log on using my site's administrator username and password. You should make sure that anonymous FTP access to your file system is disabled. In fact, once everything has been deployed and is up and running satisfactorily, you should disable your FTP account altogether until you need to make use of it again. Second, you can see that the file is being copied to the `public_html` folder. This will give the `catalog` folder a web address of `http://www.domain.com/catalog` once it is extracted on the other side.

The final point to note is that I had an estimate of about one minute for the total transfer time. This transfer was done over an ADSL line, which is fairly fast—if you don't zip the files up, you can expect a seriously long upload time because the FTP utility has to create all the files and folders itself on the destination server. Remember, that it's not only the speed of the connection, but also the speed of the FTP utility being used, that can affect upload times.

FTP Utility

Not everyone will be able to do things this way, so for those of you who cannot make use of drag-and-drop facilities, the next thing to do is make sure you have an FTP client. Linux and Windows machines all ship with one by default, so simply open up a command shell and type in the following command or its equivalent for your system:

```
c:\> ftp --help
```

This should bring up a help file, which you can browse over to get a feel for things. Now, this utility works in a fairly intuitive manner. You need to make a connection to the host, and then tell the FTP utility to send over the files you want to upload. This can be achieved in a number of ways depending on the type of FTP utility you are using—some have graphical interfaces and others don't. For the purposes of this chapter, we'll simply look at the command-line version. To log on to your site, simply enter the host name, username, and password (which should be required), as shown here:

Once you have made a connection you can simply upload the archive file to the site using the commands as shown here (these may differ depending on how your FTP utility works):

You can see that we have done the following:

- Logged on to the FTP account by supplying a username and password.
- Changed the remote working directory to public_html; this is where we would like the file to be uploaded to.
- Set the transfer type to binary, because we are uploading a .zip file and not a plain text file (which would use ascii).

Your FTP client will then let you know how things turn out, and from the screenshot you can see we get a report of success. The files have been transferred without a hitch. So far so good...

Make Sure the Host is Ready

Now, once you have uploaded your osCommerce files, you need to create a database and give an administrator access via a password. There are a number of ways this can be done in, so I will demonstrate on the demo site's hosting package one of the ways for creating a database for our store. Hopefully the process you follow will be quite similar. If you get stuck, get help from your host's support team; that's what they are there for.

The demo site has an interface for MySQL database creation, like this (you might find that your host provides something quite similar):

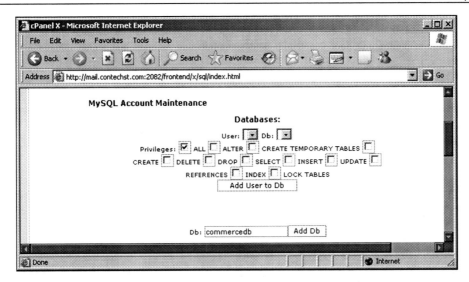

Entering a database name and clicking Add Db brings up a confirmation page. Now we have a database to work with, so we're getting somewhere. Of course, we need to specify a user for this database. The following user is created and then added to the commercedb database:

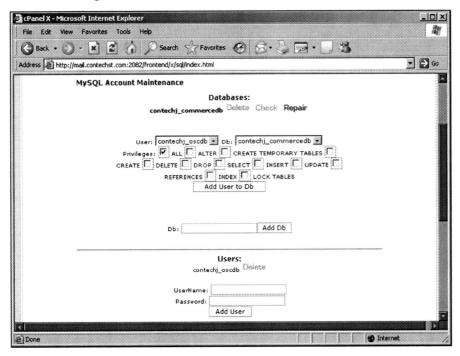

For the purposes of installing the database, we will use the oscdb user that we added to the newly create database. You're free to choose whatever username you want depending on what suits you best.

Notice in the previous screenshot that the host automatically prepends something (in this case contechj_) to all the user and database names. Your host will likely do this too if it is using a single MySQL RDBMS for multiple database accounts. If so, make a note of it, as you will need this when configuring your connection variables in osCommerce in a moment.

Perfect! We now have everything set up on the host server, so let's look at the files on our development machine and ensure they are fit to be transferred across to the host.

Installing osCommerce on the Host

Open up the ZIP file on the host machine and extract the contents to the public_html folder. Now open up your web browser, navigate to http://www.<yourdomain>.com/catalog/index.php (Remember to replace the <yourdomain> placeholder address with the domain name of your site). You should see the following screen presented there once you have done that (notice that your browser has been redirected to a slightly different URL in that we are now in the install folder):

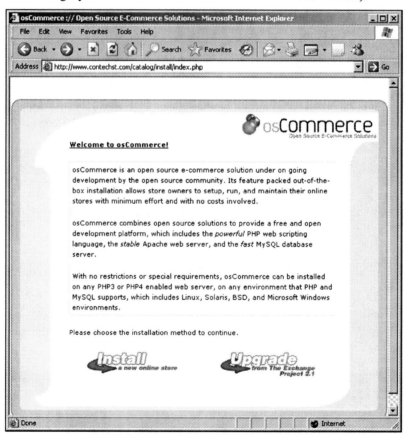

Since we desire a brand new installation, click on the left-hand option (Install a new online store) provided on the opening screen. This will bring up the next screen, which provides two options, both of which we want to ensure are selected before continuing:

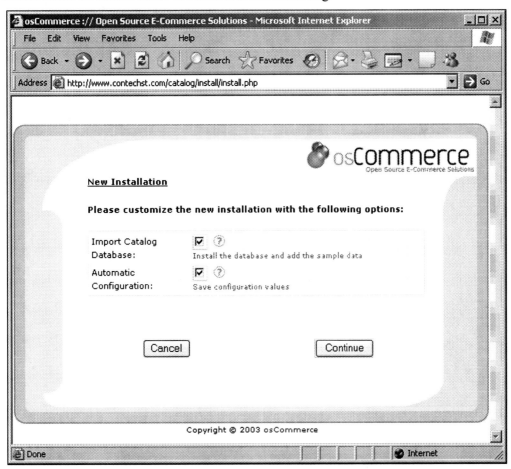

If your screen looks like the previous screenshot, then click Continue. The next page is important as it relates back to the settings we provided for MySQL earlier on in the installation procedure. Ensure that you correctly fill this out according to your set up. To give you a clue, here is how the demo site's settings were laid out:

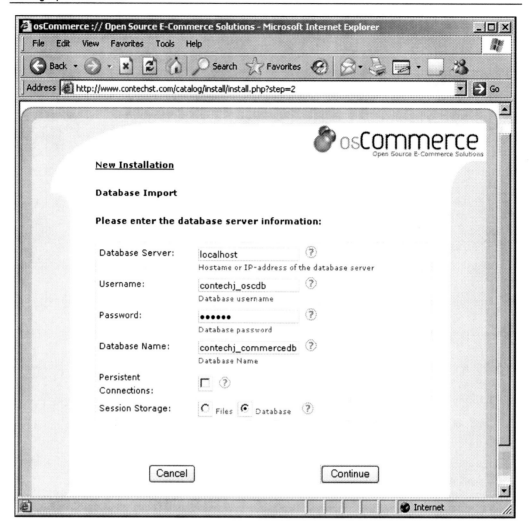

If you look at the settings made in the previous screenshot, you can tell that we have decided to use localhost as our server of choice. (You should consult your host to find out what you need to substitute in here if for some reason this does not work.) The next thing to do is supply osCommerce with a valid username and password—naturally you should make use of the ones you have just set up in the previous section.

Finally, we enter contechj_commercedb as the name of the database we would like to use when osCommerce creates all the tables it needs within MySQL—remember to use precisely the name of the database you created in the previous section.

Just to simplify our lives, we chose to have Session Storage maintained within the database as opposed to within files—there are both, pros and cons to both methods of storage, but using the database is fine for our purposes.

Click Continue once you are satisfied with your settings, and you should see a 'success' message informing you of the following:

A test connection made to the database was successful.

All good and well! Next click Continue once again to actually get osCommerce to create your database. Once it is done, it will confirm success with another message, and clicking Continue again will bring up the next step in the installation, which will display some information about your server. Please ensure this is all correct before continuing:

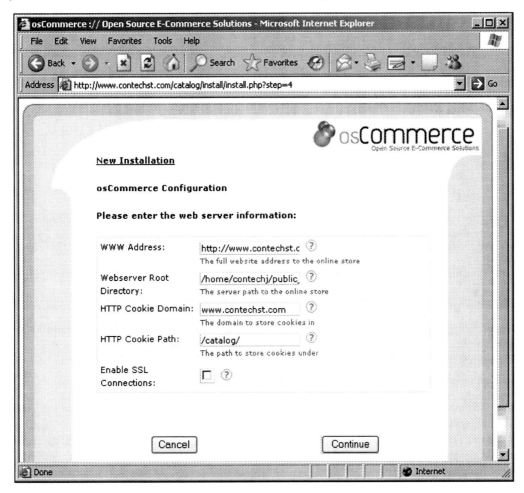

Note that at this stage we don't need SSL Connections to be enabled, so we can leave that unchecked for the time being; you will only need to worry about SSL once you come to consider your site's security. Click Continue once you are happy that the WWW Address and Webserver Root Directory are OK, and point to where your actual catalog directory can be found on your web browser (WWW

Address) and on your file system (Webserver Root Directory). Keep clicking through the remaining pages ensuring you are happy with all of the settings mentioned—there is nothing particularly important from here on until you get to the final page:

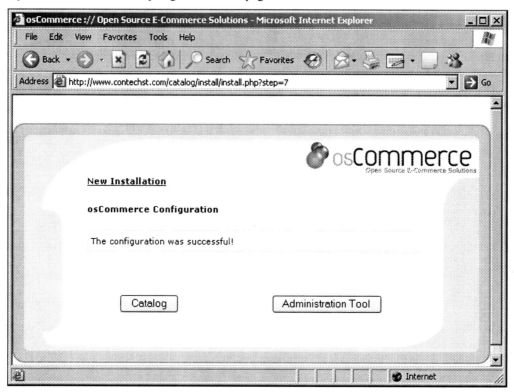

You are then presented with a 'successful installation' page, which will give you two options (as shown in the screenshot above): the first is to view the Catalog, and the second is to view the Adminstration Tool. Let's take a quick peek at those here...

Configuring osCommerce

With osCommerce installed now, one might be forgiven for breathing a huge sigh of relief because everything has been done and the universe is unfolding as it should. Of course, I urge you to click on the Catalog option on the final installation window in order to get a reality check. You will no doubt find that the page that is brought up spawns some horrid-looking warnings before actually displaying anything that could be mistaken for an online shop, much like this:

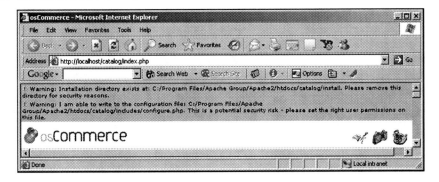

Don't worry, though! We'll quickly talk about how we can make these warnings disappear.

Some of you may have noticed that the URI in the previous screenshot says localhost instead of www.contechst.com. This is because, for the purposes of testing, much work was done on the author's own machine and not on the live site. This doesn't affect you at all and you will be able to follow along on your own hosted site regardless.

To begin with, the first warning tells us that the install directory exists within the catalog folder, and we are asked to remove this for security reasons. Well, OK! They're the boss. Navigate to the install directory on your file system and remove it from the catalog folder.

Once that is done, we can turn our attention to the next warning, which tells us that we have a potential security risk in the form of a writeable configuration file. Of course, we never, ever want anyone other than ourselves to be able to write to any configuration file on our own system, so this warning is certainly an important one.

Navigate over to the configure.php file on your file system—you can find the file by reading the warning given in the browser; it will tell you the file path of the file in question. Once there, you will need to change the permission settings of that file so that it is not writeable as shown here:

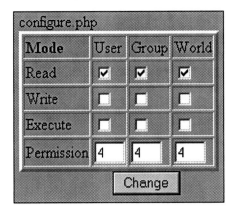

With those two configuration changes made to your osCommerce installation, I'll wager that everything is now in pretty good working order; refresh your catalog index page in your browser or navigate to http://www.<domain_name>/catalog/index.php if you have closed it down already. You should now find that you are presented with a demonstration site, which is free of any warnings (for the meantime). The index page should look like this assuming everything is working properly:

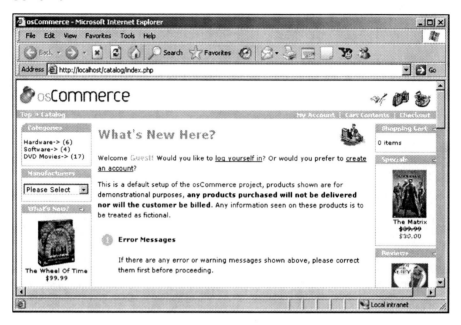

If this is the screen you have reproduced on your machine, then you can be certain that everything is shipshape and raring to go. Because osCommerce does most of its own setup, we shall not spend too much time testing everything at the moment. There is, however, a troubleshooting section at the end of this chapter, which will run through some of the more common problems that people encounter on the road to online success.

Before we do continue, though, you might well be curious to see what the administration tool looks like. If this is the case, either click the Administration Tool option given on the final page of the installation, or navigate to http://localhost/catalog/admin/index.php. In either case, you should see your admin tool, all shiny and new:

From here, you will be able to perform pretty much any administrative task your heart could desire. Everything is neatly categorized, very well laid out, and intuitive to use. We will be looking at how to customize our site in Chapter 3, where we show how to use and find your way around this impressive tool. For now though, it is good enough to know that it is there ready for use.

Troubleshooting

Very little should have gone wrong during the setup process as outlined in this chapter. However, it is not beyond the realms of possibility that things do go amiss—hopefully due to something simple (and easily rectified) like a typo. One of the most frustrating problems can occur during the final stages in the setup of osCommerce. For example, you may have come across something like this:

In this case, the first thing you need to do is click the Back button, check your settings, and try again. If this problem persists despite you being absolutely sure that you have made no mistake, then simply refresh the window before trying again.

Again, if this does not work, then you need to go back to the *Make Sure the Host is Ready* section and follow the instructions there to ensure that you do have valid database users and that they are using passwords and that they are allowed to access the *correct* database.

Finally, if there are any niggling worries (or even larger worries) that have reared their ugly heads, then this is the course of action you should take:

1. Check the documentation.
2. Visit the osCommerce site, go to the knowledge base (http://www.oscommerce .info/) or forums (http://forums.oscommerce.com), and search for similar posts or problems.
3. View the bug list (http://www.oscommerce.com/community/bugs) to see if your problem is a reported bug.

4. If you can't find similar posts or problems, then try posting your queries on the forums, and ask someone in the community to give you a hand.

5. If this does not yield a positive result, get in touch with your Internet Service Provider and see if they can guide you through the installation, or shed light on what the problem is.

6. To supplement this, get on Google and try using relevant keywords to locate a similar problem, with hopefully a solution presented.

It may seem like a bit of a cop-out to give you a list of actions to take rather than present all the problems that may crop up. However, having a solid, robust approach for finding solutions to problems is infinitely more valuable than simply being given individual solutions to a problem. The above points form a methodology that should help you solve *any* osCommerce-related problem you encounter ever—not just the ones that might be bugging you now!

Summary

By this stage you have a fully functional online store, just waiting for the development that lies ahead in the coming days, weeks, and months. Having ensured that everything is not only installed, but also working properly, you can be confident that when the time comes to sit down and begin, you won't come across any unwanted surprises.

Having also briefly discussed the various bits and bobs that could have gone wrong along the way, the main thing to remember in terms of troubleshooting is the points presented at the end of the *Troubleshooting* section. These points provide a solid method for finding a solution to any problem, and not simply those concerned with installation and setup.

With that, we are now ready to get our hands dirty and begin customizing the site.

3
Basic Configuration

Take my word, there's a fair old amount to do in terms of configuring your individual osCommerce installation to suit a new business. Fortunately, the people at osCommerce have made a lot of default choices that are pretty sensible, so provided you have a good look at everything that is up for configuration, and ensure that you understand what all the settings do and mean, quite a bit of it *can* go unchanged. Apart from actually making a decision about the multitude of settings that go into defining osCommerce's look, feel, and behavior, you also have to physically implement your choices. For this, we are given the excellent administration tool (found under the admin folder in your installation), which you can think of this as osCommerce's command center.

From the administration tool, we can perform just about any configuration task our hearts desire. I say "just about" because there are always fiddly bits that aren't easily dealt with from the standard administrative interface. Consequently, in this chapter, we won't perform every bit of configuration needed to get our site up and running—that would involve a lot of work, which we don't need to concern ourselves with until a bit later on.

Basically, in order to be as efficient as possible in terms of our overall development of the site, we are going to work with the 80/20 philosophy in mind. This means we should aim to get roughly 80% of the configuration done with about 20% of the overall effort. The remaining 20% of configuration work will get done when we look at different or specialized bits of functionality, and for that we may need specialist knowledge, third-party software, or simply more time than we want to spend on configuring our setup for the moment. So what is it precisely that we are going to get done in this chapter? Well, we are going to discuss and modify the following sections found under the Configuration tab of the administration tool:

- My Store
- Maximum and minimum values
- Images
- Customer details
- Shipping/packaging
- Product listing
- Stock

- Logging
- Cache
- Email options
- Download
- GZip compression
- Sessions

What are we *not* going to look at in this chapter? Well, we aren't going to run through each and every option available in osCommerce in detail. Many of the default settings are pretty self-explanatory, and require nothing more than a quick decision on your part. The ones that have a slightly less clear meaning or are more complex in their action will be scrutinized more closely. More or less it's fair to say that it's the default behavior of osCommerce that's going to be modified in this section of the book. Things like changing the look and feel of the site, or populating the product database are left to their own chapters a little later.

One final thing to bear in mind is that if you still, at this stage, don't have a clear idea of what you expect from your site, you will find that it is hard to make some of the decisions concerning how you want certain aspects of osCommerce to behave. Now, it is understood that sometimes it is simply not possible to know everything in advance, so you might wish to take notes of what you are and are not modifying, and what you think you will need to come back to at a later stage. Having a quick reference of what you have and haven't done at any given junction in the development phase will make your life a lot easier if you ever do need to take a step back.

Anyway, it's certainly exciting to be finally working on the actual site; so without further delay, let's begin...

The Administration Tool

Having an online tool like the one shipped with osCommerce is of great value and advantage to us osCommerce users. If, for example, you had undertaken to build your own site from scratch, then no matter how well you built your site, it would probably be prohibitive in terms of time taken to develop a fully functional online administration center to go with it. This would mean effectively that you were doomed forever to modify your database manually, or go searching for default settings within the actual pages of your code.

Thankfully, that scenario is not one we need to consider, and the only real challenges for us are to learn how to use the admin tool effectively, and to understand the behavior of all the settings. Don't be fooled, though; if we make changes to the default settings without fully understanding the consequences of the changes, there can be some unexpected and untimely surprises, and surprises in the programming world are never good! The administration tool goes a long way to helping us make our decisions though; it even provides a sentence or two outlining what each given option means—although this is often insufficient to fully appreciate the effects of changing the setting. The following screenshot shows the administration tool, open on the My Store page of the Configuration section:

All the pages in the administration tool have several common generic features, which you should be aware of. First, there is a navigation bar running along the top of the screen, which allows us to jump to the Administration home page (this option is presented again on the far right of the bar), the osCommerce homepage (Support Site), as well as our actual osCommerce site's homepage, held in Online Catalog. Nothing too life-threatening there, but useful if you want to jump around to find information, or test the results of your modifications.

Next, all the setting options that are available for us to use are categorized and stored in the box on the far left of the screen. This chapter concentrates on only the first option, Configuration, because the other options all overlap specific topics that warrant their own chapters. Clicking on a heading category—for example, Configuration—will bring up its list of options, and clicking on these subcategories will bring up a page containing all the setting options for that category.

The category setting options are displayed in the center of the screen in a tabular format, and each option is a link that will bring up its own edit option and description on the far right of the screen. So, for example, in the previous screenshot the setting we are looking at is the Store Name.

Clicking on the edit button will bring up the following page, which we can use to enter text and save the new setting:

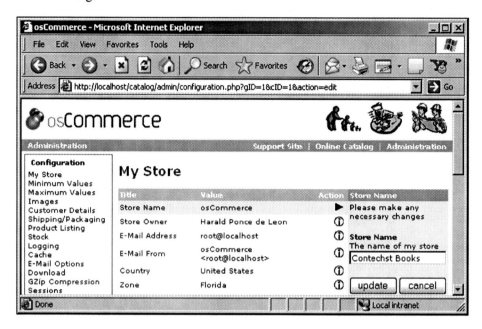

Clicking the update button will then take us back to the settings page, which should now reflect any changes we have made. That about explains how we go about configuring the site. The rest is really about understanding what effect the changes will have. Of course, as with anything, there is also a good way and a bad way to go about making changes. Most of you should be able to guess straight off that the good way will involve some sort of verification process to ensure that our changes have the desired effect.

Now, for something as simple as deciding on the store's name, there is probably little that could go wrong, so don't feel you have to waste time verifying every single change you make. However, you should make it a point to check results after a certain number of *easy* modifications, as well as verify the more complicated settings (if possible) as and when you make them.

> You should make a note (a physical one, not a mental one) of the settings you have changed in case you have to come back and fiddle around with things. Save your notes in a file called `configuration_settings.txt` and leave it in a folder entitled, for example `development_notes`, somewhere where you will find it again.

My Store

There are a few settings of interest in this section, and they warrant a fair investigation. For the most part, however, it is pretty plain sailing and there isn't too much in here that should cause stress. The first four items in the table—Store Name, Store Owner, E-Mail Address, and E-Mail

From—are reasonably straightforward to understand, although there are a few things you might want to consider before writing in your personal details.

The Store Name property will appear, among other things, in emails sent to the store owner when customers use the Contact Us page on the site. The Store Owner is most likely yourself; if you are developing for someone else, then your employer's name should go in here. Not very exciting stuff, but you will notice that the store owner's name is the name that appears in the To: field of the emails received from customers.

Talking of which, the part worth thinking about here is whether you really want all customer queries (complaints, compliments, suggestions, or anything else for that matter) to land up at your personal email. The answer is probably an emphatic "No!" So what do you do? The best way to get around this is to create an E-Mail Address on your site that is used to collect all the customer emails in one place, which you can then peruse at your leisure, or pass off to an employee, or deal with in whatever manner you choose—at least they aren't clogging up your private email inbox.

So, in this instance, it is probably best to ignore the short description of E-Mail Address (The e-mail address of my store owner) given by osCommerce, and enter an address that you have access to but is not necessarily your personal email address—in this case, I have used staff@contechst.com. If you wish to test out this functionality, then you will need to ensure that whatever address you enter is at least valid and can be accessed by you.

The following screenshot shows an email sent from a client to the store, and the reply from the store to the customer, shown below it. Take note in particular of the values in all the fields shown:

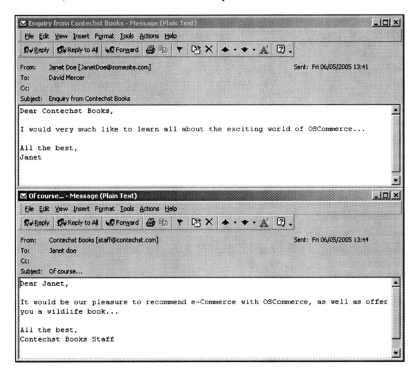

This brings up an important point, which should be mentioned before we continue:

> Just because a configurable property has a given name and description, doesn't mean you have to follow the wording precisely. It is far more important to think about *how* you want your site to work when filling in values.

Next, the Send Extra Order Email To option allows you to specify who else receives a copy of the order confirmation email sent out whenever a customer completes an order. By default this is only sent to the customer, but you may wish to set up an email address to which these order emails are sent so that you can keep track or maintain copies of orders via email—you don't *have* to do this; it is quite easy to track orders through the admin tool as well. So, assuming you have an email address orders@contechst.com, you could edit the option to send a duplicate email by typing the following in the textbox presented: Order Email <orders@contechst.com>.

At the time of writing, the Use Search-Engine Safe URLs feature was still under development, and should be left as false unless you have a newer version where this is a tried and tested feature. The Store Address and Phone option allows you to enter the details you wish to be made available to customers who are using a check or money order to pay for their goods. Apart from these options, the rest are all pretty self explanatory, and it is really up to the individual to make a decision. The following screenshot shows all the My Store settings for the demo site:

My Store

Title	Value	Action
Store Name	Contechst Books	⊕
Store Owner	David Mercer	⊕
E-Mail Address	staff@contechst.com	⊕
E-Mail From	Contechst Books <staff@contechst.com>	⊕
Country	United States	⊕
Zone	California	⊕
Expected Sort Order	desc	⊕
Expected Sort Field	date_expected	⊕
Switch To Default Language Currency	false	⊕
Send Extra Order Emails To	Order Email <orders@contechst.com>	⊕
Use Search-Engine Safe URLs (still in development)	false	⊕
Display Cart After Adding Product	true	⊕
Allow Guest To Tell A Friend	false	⊕
Default Search Operator	or	⊕
Store Address and Phone	Contechst Books 31 Wildlife Drive Wilderness California United States of America 021 555 4567	⊕
Show Category Counts	false	▶
Tax Decimal Places	0	⊕
Display Prices with Tax	false	⊕

Notice that the Default Search Operator and Show Category Counts options have had their values modified, while the Display Cart After Adding Product has been left as true—these simply reflect my personal preference for how a site should be presented, and I am quite certain that ten different people will have ten different opinions. The rest of these properties are left in your capable hands to decide on.

Maximum and Minimum Values

The maximum and minimum values deal with a variety of things ranging from governing customer information, to determining how many search results to present, to customer order history. Fortunately, most of these settings are pretty straightforward, so there isn't much that should cause problems here either. Before we show the default settings for Contechst Books, it is worth looking at a couple of things when determining the type of settings you want to put in place here.

The first thing to do is to navigate to the customer registration page, which you can reach by clicking on the create an account? link on the site's index page. This will bring up a page consisting of a list of textboxes that your customers will use to enter their information in order to create an account. It's a worthwhile exercise to actually fill this information out with legal and illegal values (illegal values are those that do not meet the stated minimum requirements in your Minimum Values configuration page) to check how your application behaves and to give you a better appreciation for the values you are setting.

For example, the minimum length of the date is given as 10 by default in the configuration section. Why ten? This is a bit strange because you only need six, or at most eight, characters to specify a date. Without looking at the create an account page, you might well change this value not realizing that osCommerce requires the user to input forward slashes to separate the days, months, and years provided in birthdates.

With that said, there is nothing we are going to modify in this section for now, since all the default minimum values represent sensible options. It is recommended, however, that you still look through each and every setting and ensure you understand what each one does, as there are still options you may wish to consider at this point. Looking at the password setting, you might consider upping the minimum length to 6 in order to encourage greater security among customers—obviously, enforcing longer passwords reduces the risk of customers' accounts being hijacked.

The Maximum Values section does not deal with customers, but with how osCommerce behaves in terms of the number of items it displays in a variety of categories. While the default settings are pretty much spot on, there are a few settings worth looking over. The first two are self explanatory, although at this stage you might not be aware that Address Book Entries refers to the fact that customers can add several addresses to their account. This allows them to specify different mailing addresses depending on where and to whom they want purchased good to go.

The Page Links value specifies the maximum number of links that will be shown on a results page. For example, if you set this to 5, then assuming you have enough products or results, you will get the following link structure:

1 2 3 4 5 [Next >>]

If you set it to 10, you would get:

1 2 3 4 5 6 7 8 9 10 [Next >>]

Categories to List Per Row might cause some confusion as it is not particularly clear what this refers to. To see how this influences your site, go to any one of the default links under the Categories section of the index page in your catalog site.

If, for example, you go to the Hardware option, you will be presented with the following screen:

The main thing to note here, though, is that there are three columns of subcategories shown. If you don't already have a window open with your Maximum Values settings page in the admin tool, then open one up and change the default value for Categories to List Per Row to 1. Refreshing the Categories page will give you the following result:

From this you can see that this setting governs how many columns are used to present the categories of products you have in your store. Simple once you know, but it can be tricky to find this out if you don't. Some things to consider when deciding on this setting are:

- How big your product category images (if any) are going to be
- How wide your page is going to be
- How many product subcategories, on average, you are going to have

Once again, the default setting is fine for the demonstration site, but this illustrates quite well that some thought should go into each and every setting—even if the end result is simply leaving the value as is.

The rest of the values in this section are pretty self explanatory, and it is left to you to go through each one and make a decision regarding what your preferences are for your own site. If you have any doubt about what a setting does, then leave it as the default. Remember, you can always come back to this section and change the values to suit your needs at any stage.

Images

Learning how to set the default values for the Images section can be a bit of a laugh. The best way to do it is to change the settings and view the results in the catalog section. Of course, ensure that you remember your default settings so that you can get things back to normal once you are done. The following screenshot shows the modified values in the Images section:

Images

Title	Value	Action
Small Image Width	10	①
Small Image Height	80	①
Heading Image Width	570	①
Heading Image Height	40	①
Subcategory Image Width	20	▶
Subcategory Image Height	57	①
Calculate Image Size	true	①
Image Required	true	①

In this case, the Small Image Width has been reduced from 100 to 10, the Heading Image Width has been increased from 57 to 570, and the Subcategory Image Width has been reduced from 100 to 20. To see the effect of these changes we will go to our catalog section and view a couple of pages. The following screenshot shows the Categories page under these modifications:

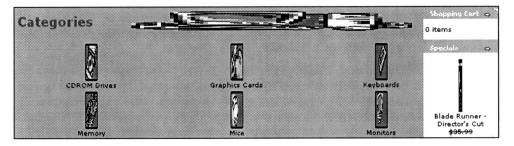

Oh dear, that's not really what we want, but it has helped to demonstrate which setting does what. The image of the Blade Runner title on the right-hand side of the screen has been squashed to only ten pixels in width—so we know how the Small Image Width affects the site. The Heading Image Width influences the image shown at the top of the page in line with the Categories title, and this image now takes up half the screen's width, which is obviously not appropriate. Finally the most obvious of the settings, the Subcategory Image Width, has been squashed to only 20 pixels, which is also not very tidy.

Playing around like this has raised some interesting questions. What size are your site's images? In other words, will they look nice with the default settings? Notice that the heading image shown in the previous screenshot is all deformed and unclear because of the stretching it has undergone. Well, it's possible that if you have made or obtained images that are of different dimensions than the default ones, then you might suffer the same fate unless you think closely about what Image values you set.

> It is possible to leave out the Width (or Height) setting for your images entirely. This will force osCommerce to size your images according to their remaining specified Height (or Width) property. Doing this should avoid any horizontal or vertical distortion as osCommerce will render the image appropriately. For this to work, the Calculate Image Size option must be set to True.

Of course, you may also decide, for example, to not have heading images at all, in which case you can leave the settings as the default ones because you will remove the images from your pages altogether when you customize your site.

Finally, it is recommended that you leave the Image Required setting as true while you are building the site, because this will allow you to spot if anything is amiss with your images—for example, if osCommerce cannot find an image, this will show up as a broken link on the screen. You can test this by modifying the name of an image in the `images` folder of your `catalog` directory and then viewing (in your browser) a page that should contain that image.

Customer Details

This is a very straightforward section, and the only setting that is modified for the demonstration site is the Company option, which has been set to false because it slows down customer registration and is not that important for our purposes. If you feel your store will benefit from knowing who your customers work for, then by all means keep it. While it is easy to understand what each setting controls in this case, you still need to think closely about what you do and don't want to store in the way of customer information.

Off the top of your head you may wonder why on earth you really need to store a customer's birthdate. After all, the more information you store about each customer, the more space you are going to use in your database. But what if down the line you decide to implement a marketing strategy that sends out a promotional discount on certain products on your customers' birthdays? Well, this is certainly a plausible marketing strategy, but one that is thoroughly impossible to implement if you haven't been storing customer birthdates from the start. The same type of argument could be made for storing gender, since certain products might be more attractive to one gender than the other, so a marketing strategy based on gender is also plausible.

At this point you should be able to see why it is so important to have a clear picture of where you want your site to go. It's a very easy slip to make saying that you don't need customer birthdates because you don't really need them at the moment. When in doubt, save the details rather than not—this will at least give you the option later on. If you know that you are really never going to use the information (like the Company value for the demo site), then remove it so as to prevent redundant data piling up in your database.

Shipping and Packaging

This section is also pretty straightforward, although there are several issues you need to make sure you are aware of before making any decisions here. The first two options, Country of Origin and Postal Code, can be dealt with pretty swiftly, but the next setting requires a bit of research. In order to Enter the Maximum Package Weight you will ship, you need to know the weight-to-cost scale of your shipping service provider, and find out what limits they have on their service.

Most good providers will have a list of all their charges, and assuming you will actually be using them often, will also have special rates and deals available to regular users. For example, `http://www.ups.com/content/us/en/shipping/time/zones/current/select.html` provides information regarding UPS's rates as well as information pertaining to their services. Whoever you choose to work with will likely have a solid support and information service to help you find your way. For example, you can find out all about costs and charges at the US Postal Service at the `http://pe.usps.gov/text/dmm/R700.htm#xih82834` page, which highlights the costs of mailing packages of different weights and sizes.

Obviously, it is imperative that you look at a shipping provider of your choice in order to work out what your expenses are going to be, as well as the most cost-effective and efficient solution for your business. Once you know how your shipping service will work (for example, whether you are going to use a daily or weekly pick-up service, whether you are going to get a special deal on international shipments, and so on), you can determine what settings are right for you.

Of course, the values you set are in pounds, and you should be aware of how much your packaging itself is going to weigh. The Package Tare Weight allows you to set a minimum value for the packaging (or throw-away) weight. If a package is large, then it is conceivable that you need to set the weight of the packaging as a percentage of the package weight instead of a single value. In such a case, osCommerce uses the percentage value given in the Larger packages – percentage increase option. The default sets the tare weight at 3 pounds and the percentage at 10, which means that for packages heavier than 30 pounds, the *percentage* value is the one which is used to calculate the package weight.

In the case of the demo site's settings, the Package Tare Weight is set to 2 pounds, and the Larger packages – percentage increase value is changed to 5 with the Maximum Package Weight being left at its default value. This means that for packages of 40 pounds or less, we are confident that only a maximum of two pounds of packaging is required—for anything above 40 pounds, we will use the percentage calculation. This is reasonable in our case since books need very little in the way of specialized packaging.

Product Listing

This section controls how you intend your products to be viewed on the site. Pretty much anything and everything from whether you actually want to display a product image at all, to whether you want to display its name or the name of the manufacturer, gets done here. This is a straightforward section with no difficult options to research—or so it would seem. Of course, depending on what you are selling, you might want different properties for your products altogether. By this I mean that if you are a book retailer, then it is unlikely you want to mention Display Product Manufacturer Name at all, but rather Display Product **Publisher** Name, or something to that effect.

Oh dear! What are we going to do if the actual properties we are configuring are not even the correct ones? Well, the quick answer is that we will get to a stage a little later on where we can configure our product attributes, among other things—and of course, we'll cheat by exploiting the difference between what we as the site's administrators see in the admin tool, and what the customer viewing the catalog sees!

The following screenshot shows the settings for the demo site:

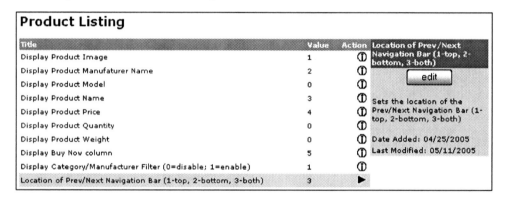

Looking through the settings shown in the previous screenshot, you can see that we want to display, in order, the product image, the manufacturer's name, the product's name, its price, and finally the Buy Now button. You might be asking yourself why—if it has already been mentioned that, as a book retailer, we don't want to Display Product Manufacturer Name—we are putting it in the line-up. The answer to this has presented itself almost too perfectly—look at the Display Product Manufacturer Name line closely in the previous screenshot. You will notice there is a spelling mistake. However, look at the results of these settings in the catalog:

Let's See What We Have Here   Show: [All Manufacturers ▾]

Displaying 1 to 3 (of 3 products)   Result Pages: 1

	Manufacturer	Product Name +	Price	Buy Now
	Warner	Beloved	$54.99	**Buy Now!**
	Fox	Courage Under Fire	~~$30.99~~ $29.99	**Buy Now!**
	Warner	Red Corner	$32.00	**Buy Now!**

Displaying 1 to 3 (of 3 products)   Result Pages: 1

You will notice that the column heading Manufacturer is spelled correctly. This means that what is shown on the screen is not directly linked to the name given for a property in the admin tool. So, we can choose to show the manufacturer in our product listing, but this does not mean we have to make the column heading in the catalog site Manufacturer; we could, if we were so inclined, change it to Publisher. This, however, will come a bit later on in the story. What's more important than this for now is that you have related the settings made to the product listing on the site page.

The final two settings are slightly different in that they deal more with navigation than anything else. Notice in the admin tool that Display Category/Manufacturer Filter is set to 1. The resulting filter when enabled in this manner is shown above the product listing in line with Let's See What We Have Here. It is a good idea to include this, as people often have some sort of brand loyalty and would wish to search your catalog for specific brands.

Finally, Location of Prev/Next Navigation Bar is set to 3. Why have we done this, and what is the 'prev/next navigation bar'? Well, when you get round to populating your database and enter the multitude of goodies you have for sale, you will get to a stage where the number of products in a category is greater than the number of products you are willing to display on the page. Incidentally, we have already set the number of items to display per page property in the Search Results setting in the Maximum Values section.

Once that happens, the navigation bar (which at present only displays Displaying 1 to 3 (of 3 products)) will be the customer's method of hopping from one page in the product listing to another. Now, I don't know about you, but I hate scrolling down to the bottom of a page only to find that I have to go right back to the top to click on the Next page link. Conversely, if I only want to look at the first couple of items and then go to the Next page, I certainly don't want to be forced to scroll to the bottom to do so. Setting this property to 3 ensures that you will make it easier for your customer to navigate your product listings by having a navigation bar at the top *and* bottom of the page.

Stock

Deciding how you want osCommerce to deal with your stock is a very tricky business, and you will be forced to do a bit of soul searching before defining the settings in this section. Ensuring that you have a coherent game plan when it comes to dealing with stock levels and how your application deals with these stock levels is paramount to the perceived and actual integrity and reliability of your system. If you are selling products that are not in stock, and are unable for some reason to fulfill your orders... Well, I don't need to continue on with the type of things *word of mouth* will spread about your store.

With that in mind, let's take a quick look at what the demo site's settings are:

Stock

Title	Value	Action
Check stock level	true	▶
Subtract stock	true	①
Allow Checkout	true	①
Mark product out of stock	Temporarily out of Stock	①
Stock Re-order level	5	①

What do these settings mean in terms of how osCommerce will behave when a customer is purchasing an item? OK, the Check stock level setting simply means that osCommerce will retrieve the number of items in stock before the customer checks out. The Subtract stock setting means that once items are purchased, the database is updated by subtracting the number of items purchased from the number of items in stock. Obviously you should be able to see that this effectively automates your stock control on the purchasing side of things.

The tricky bit is the Allow Checkout setting. Since we have set Check stock level to true, osCommerce is aware of how much stock is available when a customer attempts to make a purchase. Setting Allow Checkout to true is taking a bit of a risk because it is saying that I, as the retailer, am confident that I can ship the purchased product on time despite the fact it is not in stock at the moment. Since the demo site relies on Packt's ability to ship product, we have gone with true in this instance because Packt's business model is such that they can deliver books very quickly.

You really need to determine whether you can do the same for all of your products before setting this to true. Some people may view this as a trade-off. In other words, do you make a loss from not selling the product, or do you risk having to refund the customer if you can't get stock in quickly enough. From a business perspective, this is not particularly sound reasoning since your value as a business stems partly from your reputation of reliability. This is not worth trading on, so rather take the hit from a direct loss of sales instead of proving to be unreliable and endeavor to improve your stock control.

The final two settings are pretty easy to understand, and are not life-threatening in any way. You can choose these to best suit you with little effort. The following screenshot shows how these settings influence the behavior of osCommerce when ordering products that have low stock. Take note of the Temporarily out of Stock message, and the notes below the product which informs the customer of their choice to continue with checkout because of our Allow Checkout setting:

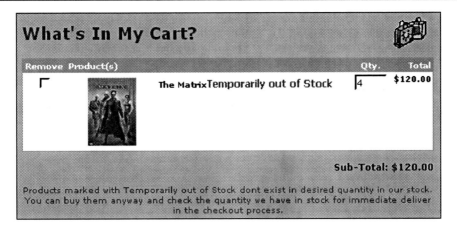

Of course, if we had set the Allow Checkout setting to false, then the second line of the checkout message would have read:

Please alter the quantity of products marked with (Temporarily out of Stock), Thank you

That all for now! We say goodbye to stocks until the next chapter, when we begin dealing with data.

Logging

Logging can be a very useful, if not critical, tool for maintaining a system's health. Logs can be used to record just about any action or change in state of an application. Most changes within an application are really of no interest to the average person, but certain things *are* useful to record in case you need that information at a later stage. Like any good system, osCommerce gives us options to create and monitor certain actions within our application. This ability comes with a caveat, however. If left untended, logs can become resource hogs, taking up gigabytes of space in a surprisingly short amount of time.

Accordingly, you need to decide what information you want to record, and then work out a good management strategy for maintaining that information. Also, logs should be kept in a secure place—you don't really need to air your database query history to the world, or worse, have it modified by someone. The options presented to us by osCommerce, along with the settings used for the demo site, are shown here:

Logging

Title	Value	Action
Store Page Parse Time	true	ⓘ
Log Destination	/home/contechj/log/page_parse_time.log	ⓘ
Log Date Format	%d/%m/%Y %H:%M:%S	ⓘ
Display The Page Parse Time	true	ⓘ
Store Database Queries	false	▶

After browsing around the site a bit, we can look at what is created in the designated log file to see the type of information we are storing. To be honest, this information is not really relevant to you at the moment, so unless there is a reason for recording logs during the configuration and customization phase, you can do without it altogether for now:

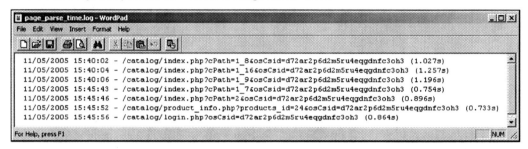

It is recommended that you leave the Store Database Query setting as false all the time unless you have a really good reason for needing it, and you know exactly how you are going to deal with all the information being stored. These logs can grow very quickly and take up a lot of space, causing problems for your site's performance if you're not careful.

Finally, remember to make a note of all the settings, in this case the log-file path, which you will need to change come deployment time, and add the files to the development_notes folder, which you created earlier.

Cache

A cache is implemented as a directory of web pages, which are held separately from the rest of the pages. The purpose of this cache is to allow the server to quickly serve cached pages instead of querying for the page afresh each time it is requested. This has implications for the speed of delivery of pages and therefore impacts positively on the customer's experience. It is recommended that you *do* use caching on your live site for this reason.

During development, however, it's not a good thing, because we want to see the results of changes (configuration or customization, or straightforward hacking) that we make to our pages every time we load them. Using a cached version of a page might not reflect the changes we have implemented, as that page would not been refreshed yet. This can often cause confusion and frustration, so for now, leave the cache entirely.

Once you are happy that the site is complete and that *all* your testing is done, you can switch caching on. To do so, simply set the Use Cache value to true, and pick a folder to save the files— by default this is /tmp/.

Email Options

Try this! Go to the last option in the administration tool, Tools, click on the Send Email option, and send an email to whatever customer you have on your site (If you don't have one, then create an account by registering on your site). Ensure before doing this that the customer you are sending the email to has an email address that *you* can receive, because you are going to test whether or not osCommerce is able to send emails with its default configuration. If not, you will need to go back to the Customers option and edit the email address for the customer appropriately.

Once you have sent the email, hang around for a bit to see if you receive it in good order. If so, then you can pretty much leave the email settings as they are for the time being. The only thing you need concern yourself with regards to email is whether your site is hosted on a Linux server (very likely) or a Windows server. If it's Linux, then you can probably leave the site as is; if it's Windows, you will probably need to change the first two settings—E-mail Transport Method and E-mail Linefeeds—to their alternative settings.

The Use MIME HTML when sending Emails option should be left as false for the moment. Obviously at a later stage you might decide you would like to spruce up your emails with some HTML, but for the moment there is no need. Remember, however, that not all mail-client applications support HTML, so you might be marginalizing some customers by using this. The good news is that as time goes by, more and more people will be able to receive MIME format emails—as opposed to just *the majority* for the moment.

You might decide that you want to check whether your customers are supplying you with email addresses that actually exist. If this is the case, then you should set the Verify E-mail Addresses Through DNS setting to true. osCommerce will then check with the relevant domain server to ensure that the given email address exists on that server and so will be able to receive the email that you are attempting to send.

You can also disable email sending entirely if you wish. For the moment this is not necessary, because at some stage we will need to test certain things relating to emails—for example, whether osCommerce is sending confirmation of order emails, and so on. It is entirely likely that you will be developing osCommerce with live data further down the line; in other words, data that reflects real live customer's details. In this case, it is unlikely that we would want them to receive erroneous emails as the result of our testing, so we simply set the Send E-Mails option to false.

If your initial attempt at sending an email didn't pay off, then try swapping the Email Transport Method setting and resending. If this fails, then I am afraid it is time for you to put the osCommerce community to good use—think of any problems like this as a chance to learn how to use the osCommerce community resource.

Download

Now we come to my personal favorite—the downloads section! One of the true wonders of the world is that we can now generate money by simply transferring information without the need for a physical medium. To this end, the demo site has a section where ebooks and articles are available for purchase and download from the site. Obviously, if you are going to be retailing products that are available for download, such as software or ebooks, then this section is of particular interest to you. If not, then feel free to leave the settings as they are and continue.

To begin with, Enable Downloads should be set to true. The rest of the other settings can be left as they are for the time being. In order to demonstrate how this now works, we will need to add a product to our product database quickly. Go to the Catalog heading option and then navigate through Categories/Products till you get to the Strategy category of the Software products—it doesn't really matter where you add a product; if you feel like adding one somewhere else, go ahead—it will make no difference.

Here you should click on the new product button, and fill out the form for a new product. For this example, the new product is called My Download in order to distinguish it from the other products, as shown here:

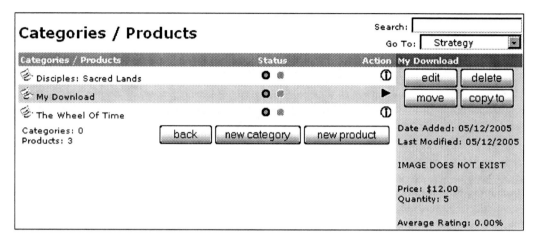

Notice the properties of My Download in the box on the right of the screen—these are arbitrary settings, and you can put in whatever you like. There is no need to hunt for an image here; this is just a quick and nasty demonstration.

Now, downloadable products in osCommerce are held in the download folder under the catalog directory, so we will need to place a file in here so that osCommerce is able to provide customers with something to download. It doesn't matter what we use for this example, but obviously when it comes to real downloads you will most likely have a zipped file with the same name as your product. In other words, if a customer downloads a computer game called unreal tournament, you will probably name your zipped download file unreal_tournament.zip to make it easy to track which files are supposed to be downloaded.

For our purposes we simply need to show that a file can be downloaded, so in this case we are going to copy account.php from the catalog folder into download. You can place any file you like in download folder, and we will attach that file to the product in the Products Attributes section in a moment. Now that the product is registered in the database, and the product file is present in the download folder, we need to set some of its attributes. For this, click on the Products Attributes link in the left-hand box of the admin tool.

At the bottom of the screen under the Products Attributes section, you will notice a drop-down list from which to select products. Find My Download from that list, add in the settings that are appropriate to the file you have placed in the download folder, and insert the product. For this example, the page looks like this:

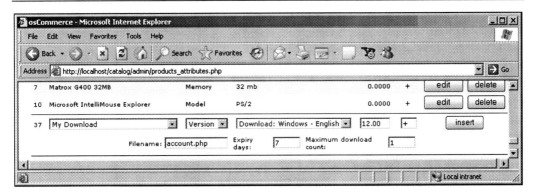

Once the product has been inserted, we can shop for it as normal on the site. If you haven't already created a customer account on the website, you will need to do so in order to be able to purchase this product. However, if you navigate to the product category in which you added the My Download product, you will notice that it is now available for purchase just like any other product. Go ahead and buy it as you would on any other site. You should end up with a page like this:

Clicking on the My Download link will allow you to begin the product download. That's all there is to it. If you are unable to download the file, then the first thing to do is check the permission settings on the pub and download folders. For Linux users, pub and download permissions should be set to 777 and 755 respectively, for Windows users, simply ensure there is no Read-Only setting in the folder properties.

You may or may not have noticed that since we have not dealt with how to set up proper payments, osCommerce has made these downloads available to use while our purchase orders are still pending. Since we haven't used a credit card, this means that the download came *before* the payment. Not a very satisfactory state of affairs at the moment, but this will all be rectified a little later on in Chapter 7, when we use a community contribution to sort things out properly. For now, though, we are able to download products if needs be.

GZip Compression

GZipping is really a good way to reduce your usage of bandwidth. Basically it allows osCommerce to send compressed files over to the customer's browser, where they are rendered as normal. Most browsers support this feature, so you should not have too many problems with compatibility if you decide to enable this setting. The only thing to look out for here is whether your server supports Zlib, and is using a version of PHP later than 4.0.4. Incidentally, if you ever need to find out how your server is configured, this simple PHP script will help you out:

```
<?
phpinfo();
?>
```

Give the script a name and navigate to it in your browser, and it will automatically print out a list of all the configuration settings (alternatively, click on Server Info in the Tools section of the admin tool). This is useful if, for example, you need to find out whether your server supports Zlib.

The Compression Level default setting is 5, and this is fine for use in general, so unless you specifically want to play around to measure performance differences, it is recommended that you leave it as is if you are going to use it. Remember that some browsers might run into problems if you enable compression, so be wary of this when your site goes live and ensure that it works through a number of different browser types.

Sessions

Sessions can be a complicated beast to understand. The 5¢ simple explanation is that sessions are what PHP uses to retain the state of a web application. What this means is that when a customer logs on to your website, PHP assigns him or her something called a session. This session holds information about this user and allows osCommerce to keep track of various important things. For example, without the use of session, how would osCommerce know which user was using which shopping cart? Since all users have their own chosen products added to their cart, osCommerce needs to be able to tell which user is which so that it can display the correct cart for each user.

This is obviously a critical function of an e-commerce site, because where money is involved, it is paramount that the right information is recorded for each transaction. In this case a transaction could mean anything from clicking on a link to purchasing a product.

Since sessions are such a critical part of osCommerce, some thought needs to go into how you want to configure your session support. We originally asked osCommerce to use database-based session support, so the first setting in the Sessions section should not affect you. If you have configured osCommerce for file-based session support, then simply set this option to the file where you would like osCommerce to record session information. You should keep this folder in your home directory for reasons of security.

The Force Cookie Use option determines whether or not we want to use cookies. Cookies are small files that are stored on the customer's browser. The information in these files can then be used for a host of different things, including making sessions more secure. The problem is that over the years many people have abused the use of cookies to the extent that a lot of people disable their use on their browsers.

If you feel you require cookies for your sessions, then osCommerce automatically inserts a page explaining to customers why and how they should enable cookies if it detects a browser that doesn't allow their use. For the moment, though, we can leave this setting as false because it is useful for us to view session information in the URL during development. Once your site is ready to go live, you will most likely want to make use of cookies.

While we haven't got to the stage of worrying about securing our site using SSL and many other wondrous things, it is worth discussing the Check SSL Session ID option briefly. Unless you have got SSL enabled on your site, you cannot set this value to true for the moment, but it is worth considering the performance versus security trade-off here. Enabling this setting means that osCommerce must check and validate the customer's session ID on every page call. This increases security because it helps prevent someone else sneaking in and hijacking a session, but, because of the extra work involved, it slows down your site slightly. However, assuming that the performance degradation is acceptable, it is generally wiser to opt for higher security—it's really a case of "better safe than sorry!"

Check User Agent is simply another option that adds to the security of your osCommerce transactions. Enabling this forces osCommerce to check the customer's user agent for each page request. The user agent is simply a string that identifies the requesting browser to the server, so checking this every time can increase security; if you have a hijacked session, it is likely (but not definite) that the user agent of the hijacker is different.

The Check IP Address option does pretty much the same thing as Check User Agent, only this time it looks at the customer's computer's IP address. The IP address of a computer is a unique string of digits which identifies a given computer. Due to the way some Internet Service Providers designate IP addresses, enabling this setting may cause some unwanted problems for some people—AOL customers in particular are susceptible to this.

The Prevent Spider Session option is an interesting one. This basically stops automated programs from setting up a working session in osCommerce by not issuing them with a session ID. Obviously an automated program is not a real live customer, so wasting resources on tracking its passage over the site is a pretty futile thing to do; after all, it's not like it's going to buy anything. Accordingly, it is recommended that you set this option to true.

Finally, the Recreate Session option will force osCommerce to recreate a session ID whenever a customer performs a logon or a checkout. This can help to prevent customers logging into each others accounts.

For the demo site under development, the following session settings were made:

Sessions

Title	Value	Action
Session Directory	/tmp	ⓘ
Force Cookie Use	False	ⓘ
Check SSL Session ID	False	ⓘ
Check User Agent	False	ⓘ
Check IP Address	False	ⓘ
Prevent Spider Sessions	True	ⓘ
Recreate Session	True	▶

Once you have decided what settings you want, record them in your development notes for later. Once you have looked at some security issues presented in Chapter 7 you will be better equipped to come back and decide exactly what you want here.

Summary

It is at this point that I should confess that I have lied to you ever so slightly. Recall that our aim in this chapter was to get 80% of the configuration done for only 20% of the effort; well, that's not really what has happened. There are quite a few more tasks to perform before we can consider the site to be more or less configured—we have done maybe 50-60% in reality, with many of the settings subject to change once you have finished testing and so on. That's not to say you should get despondent about how much further there is to go, because there have been some very valuable lessons learned in this chapter for very little effort.

What we have done is gone through the very basic and most general settings, which in turn has forced us to think about how we want our osCommerce application to behave in the end, which is always a worthwhile exercise. This is extremely important, as you have now been exposed to the type of things one needs to contemplate before making decisions that influence the running of the site. Furthermore, you have seen how to relate the changes in settings to the changes customers will see. Also not to be ignored is the newly learned ability to make use of the administration tool, which will form a big part of the site's development and administration in the future.

The rest of the configuration settings coincide with more specific development tasks—such as populating our product database and implementing payment facilities—and as a result are going to be discussed in their specific chapters. But for now you should feel safe in the knowledge that you have learned much about the way in which osCommerce works, and have (hopefully) built up a set of development notes that will help you pinpoint the settings to be looked at before you announce the site to the public.

4
Working with Data

Data is the heart of any application that needs to retain or manipulate information in any way. How to go about storing information in a database is generally a cause of consternation for developers building applications from scratch. The problem, you see, is that unlike any other part of a program, which can generally be used with little to no modification for other applications, databases must be tailored precisely to their specific application in order to be effective. You don't need to worry about this though; it's all taken care of already.

As you know, osCommerce sites use the **MySQL Relational Database Management System** to store information about products, customers, sessions, languages, configuration, orders, reviews, specials, and a bunch of other things. The structure of the database is created and built during the installation process and is ready to work whenever you decide to make changes. In fact, we have already been working with data because the configuration properties set in the last chapter are, of course, all retained by storing them in the database.

In this chapter, we are going to be working on adding, removing, and updating business-related information in the database. What type of information is this? Well, for a start, we need to learn how to add and remove customers, their orders, and most importantly, products to and from the database. Discussing how to add and remove products will take up the bulk of this chapter simply because it is more than likely the type of data you will work with most often.

It must be said—despite its apparent obviousness—that ensuring your data is accurate is just about the most important thing you can do, because corrupt data is worse than worthless, it's actually detrimental. So, along the way, we will talk about the right approach to dealing with your information. This is important because, believe it or not, it is actually quite simple to produce data that is not accurate.

Specifically, in this chapter, we are going to talk about:

- The preparations involved before adding products
- Adding, removing, and updating data from the Catalog, Customers, and Reports sections in the administration tool
- Viewing reports

Finally, it is important to realize that while it is essential that you understand how to use the administration tool effectively in order to build and maintain your site, it is not the be all and end all. You are encouraged to look for contributions such as EasyPopulate, or third-party tools like phpMyAdmin, which can help sort out your data problems in a more efficient manner than simply using the admin tool.

Preparing to Add Product Data

Many of you will already have a list, or at least a partial list, of all the products you intend to sell via your website. You may be an established business with a full catalog that you need to enter into your osCommerce site, or you could have a single product to begin with that you want to sell. Whatever your situation, there are certain things that you will need to get in order before you can create an online catalog that will actually promote the sale of your goods. So what are these things? Well, the best way to find out is to let osCommerce answer that.

Open up the administration tool to the Catalog section, choose the Categories/Products link and navigate all the way down till you reach a product, and click edit—it doesn't matter which product for the moment. You will be presented with a screen that looks something like this:

Looking up and down this page you can see that there are a number of *properties* assigned to this product. Most are pretty intuitive to deal with; Products Status is easy enough to decide, and the Date Available also should not present you with too many difficulties. If you set the Date Available property to some time in the future, then a friendly note pops up on the product's page on the website informing the customer that This product will be in stock on Friday 21 October, 2005 (or something similar depending on the date you set).

Of course, with the Out of Stock option set, the website will not show any product at all.

Products Manufacturer is an interesting attribute in the case of the demo site. We don't want to list the manufacturers for our products, but we require the publishers to be listed. However, rather than redesigning the internals of osCommerce to represent this requirement, we can replace Manufacturer with Publisher in our mind's eye and simply add publishers' names to our list of manufacturers so that they can be displayed on the site as normal.

In order to add a manufacturer, you would simply go to the Manufacturers tab in the Catalog section and add one from there. All this will all be discussed in detail once we get to the *Catalog* section later in this chapter, so don't worry about it for the moment.

Products name, Tax Class, Products Price (Net), Products Price (Gross), and Products Description are also pretty straightforward. Of course, you will need to research whatever special tax requirements you may be subject to before you go ahead and set that information. The default on the site, which is set in the Locations/Taxes section, is left for the time being since the product shown is not the one that the demo site will sell. We will deal with the tax options later on in Chapter 6. For now though, simply be aware that you will need to know where you stand with taxes in order to make the right choices when it comes to adding products.

Another interesting thing to note here is the fact that everything is, by default, given in three languages. If you think that you will need to include more than English into your site then obviously you will have to either hire someone to do the translations for you, or if you are a polyglot, you can simply copy out the product info into the language of your choice. Setting the languages you would like to use gets taken care of by the Localization section of the administration tool, and this will be dealt with in the chapter on customization. If you are only going to sell to a predominantly English-speaking customer base, then simply leave the other language options blank.

Take a look at the Products Description text area on your own product page. You should notice that there are HTML formatting tags in this text. This is because osCommerce will render whatever you enter into this text area directly to the browser. Without adding the relevant HTML formatting you could be left with descriptions that aren't nicely laid out—in this instance, the <br> tags simply give each sentence a new line.

Products Quantity is simple enough, and osCommerce will automatically reduce this when there are purchases if you have enabled stock control (see the previous chapter for more info on this). The Products Model gets displayed in the site's navigation breadcrumb bar. So whatever you would like to show in the navigation bar is what you should enter here. For example, changing the model to Frantic_DVD will produce the following breadcrumb trail when viewed on the site. The Product Model is a very important value and you should ensure that it is never left blank and is always unique:

With that done, you can turn your attention to the Products Image and the Products URL. Now, we will be dealing with images in detail in the next chapter, so don't fret too much about this. However, recall our earlier discussion about how osCommerce is laid out; because of the way things are set up, osCommerce automatically looks in the `images` folder under `catalog` for its images. It is recommended that you look at how the default image structure is laid out, and select one that will suit your store (there will be recommendations made in the following chapter).

Setting the Products URL will give customers the option to visit the product maker's website while viewing the product information in your store. Leaving this blank will simply cause the option not to be presented. Finally, Products Weight is easy enough to deal with, given suitable scales to measure it with.

Now that you have a good idea of what information you need to gather on each of your products and how to categorize them, we can begin adding to the store.

Catalog

The Catalog section of the administration tool is a pretty nifty piece of content management software. You can control your stock with a fine tooth comb from here, and although it is not complete on its own, using some of the community contributions to extend the default functionality provided should give you all the help you need to run and maintain the stock on your site; as mentioned, you may wish to look at EasyPopulate in order to upload a number of products at once.

Before we begin by looking at the subsections of the Catalog administration tool, there are a few things that you should know beforehand. Above and beyond the standard functionality provided, osCommerce also gives you a drop-down navigation list to help find your way around your data directory structure, as well as a search tool. If you open up the Catalog page, you will be presented with something like this:

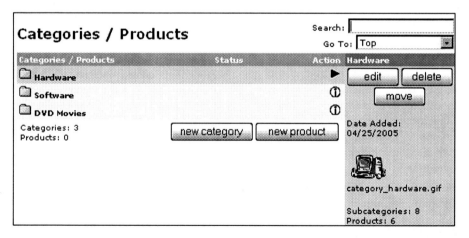

Use the Search textbox (type in the name of the product or category and hit *Enter*) to find products or categories quickly, or use the drop-down list to navigate to various sections without having to click on the individual category links. Apart from this, you should be familiar with the way the tool works from your experience while configuring osCommerce. Let's go ahead and look through each of the sections in the Catalog section.

Categories/Products

You should ensure that you have a clear idea of what your directory structure looks like as well where your products are going to fit within that structure before you begin adding products. Assuming you do, we can go ahead and make that structure a reality by adding some data. However, we won't show more than a product or two since we have not dealt with the subject of images, which are obviously a fairly important part of the site.

Adding and Deleting Categories and Products

Click on the new category button to add your new categories in the Categories/Products section of the Catalog folder in the admin tool. You will notice that you have the option to fill in the Sort Order while adding the new category. Adding an integer here will define where in the navigation list the current entry should appear. Leaving this blank means that osCommerce will sort the categories in alphabetic order. For example, Contechst Books wishes the e-Books and Documents category to appear last, so it is given a high sort order while the other categories are left blank.

Once you have defined all your categories—including adding subcategories by navigating to a category and clicking the add category button to add a new folder there—check your site to view the changes made. The demo site at this stage looks like this:

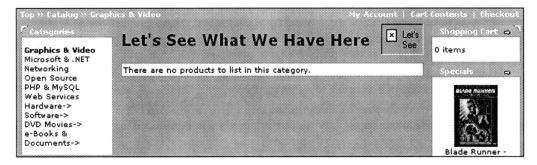

There are several things to note here. First, the new categories and subcategories have been added (you can tell that e-Books & Documents has subcategories because of the arrow to the right of the title) and that obviously, there are as yet no products in the Graphics & Video section, which is the currently selected category. Secondly, you will notice a broken picture link to the immediate left of the shopping-cart box. This is because we have not yet added any category images to the images folder. You may even decide to do away with these images altogether, so wait until next chapter where they are covered in detail before making a choice.

Notice also that we have not yet gotten rid of the default categories. This is because removing all these products now will leave us with a pretty dismal looking website and make it harder to ascertain what changes have had what effect and where. There's no rush to remove them for the moment, so leave them as they are for now.

Next, let's add a new product to the database. Go to a product category and click on new product. This will bring up the product's buying info page, which we discussed earlier. Fill out the details of the product and click preview; you will then be shown what your product listing will look like on the site. For example, we have added a book entitled VirtualDub Video: Capture, Processing and Encoding with all its accompanying details. The result on the site is:

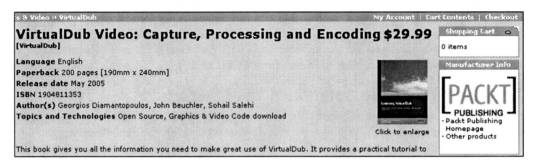

From this you should be able to tell the following:

- A small image for the product has been uploaded here. Assuming you haven't uploaded an image file for the product you will have a broken link instead.

- HTML formatting tags have been used to lay out the information nicely. For example, the book's specification information has been bolded using the <b> and </b> tags, and blank lines have been inserted using the <br> tag. All in all, the effect is pretty striking. If you want to try some special effects, remember that you have a stylesheet, which you can use to fiddle around with, and if you wish to learn more about HTML, search Google with the term HTML example.

- The Products Model has been entered as VirtualDub; you can see this by looking at the breadcrumb at the top left of the page.

- If you look closely, you will note that a manufacturer image (Packt Publishing), shown in the Manufacturer Info box on the left, has also been added.

That is really all there is to adding products to the database. Of course, you can remove them just as easily by clicking the delete button on the products administration page. This is how the new products administration page looks:

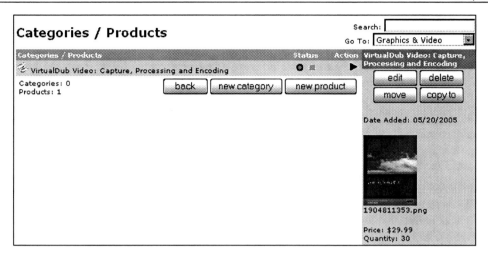

Notice that there are now two more buttons available apart from edit and delete that you are already familiar with. These two options relate to where and how the product is stored and accessed in the database, and we'll look at these in a moment.

Along with all the buttons are two 'lights' under the Status heading towards the middle of the screen. These are used to activate and deactivate products without having to go through the trouble of adding them or removing them from the database. So, if there is a product that you don't want to make available on the site for some reason, but you also don't want to play around with its settings, you can simply set it to inactive by clicking on the pink button.

Moving and Copying Categories and Products

Let's say that it so happens that the *VirtualDub* title is available for download (it isn't, but let's just assume that it is). This being the case, it would make sense to have it appear under the e-Books & Documents folder too. Now, we don't really want to navigate to that category and re-enter all that information, so rather than that, simply click on copy to, and the following options are presented:

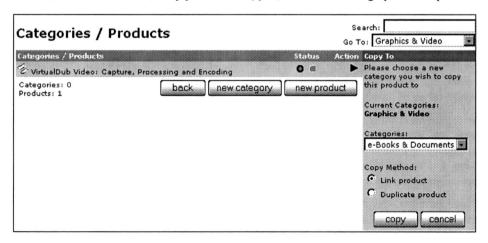

Now we can choose whether or not to Duplicate product, which will create an entirely new record in the database under the stipulated category, or alternatively, choose Link product, which will simply link the product to the stipulated category. Since we don't want to create unnecessary redundant data it is a far better idea to link the product than duplicate it. Doing this means that when we navigate to the e-Books and Documents category on the site, we are presented with the same VirtualDub product.

This has quite far-reaching consequences for stock control because if you choose to duplicate the product you now have to worry about two sales channels for the same products and ensure that you have enough stock for both. If you simply link the product then you only have one product being sold and your stock control continues as normal.

The other option, move, will simply move that product to the category of your choice. The product then no longer exists in its original place, but only in the new category. This example should have highlighted the fact that sometimes you need to think closely about whether to link, duplicate, or move a product because it may be necessary to set the weight property of the product to 0 in order to make it downloadable. In this case, duplicating the data and modifying the Product's Weight property in the duplicated version is probably the best option.

It should be mentioned that you can also move categories although you aren't able to use copy to. For categories, move works in exactly the same way as for products, by simply adding the category entry to the target category and removing it from the present one. It is recommended that you experiment with these features since there are other default behaviors you should learn about. For example, what happens if you try to move a product to a folder that already contains that product?

Product Attributes

Don't get the product attributes confused with the properties we covered in the *Preparing to Add Product Data* section earlier. What we have looked at is effectively the 'buying information' that is used to inform customers about a product on the website. The product attributes that we will look at later deal with a different type of information. For example, in the last section there was no way to indicate whether the product you added was available for download.

Depending on what it is you are selling you will obviously need different product attributes to be reflected in your application. For example, should you wish to become the largest retailer of Bonsai trees in the northern hemisphere, it is unlikely the default attributes of color, size, model, Memory, and version will be of much use to you. By the same token, making up a couple of categories on the fly will probably also not help because there are a few tricks up osCommerce's sleeve that should be exploited—we will come to this while looking at how to use the Product Attributes section of the administration tool in a little while.

Assuming you were the aforementioned horticulturalist, then product attributes such as species, style, and age are probably of more use to you because they apply directly to the type of product you are selling. Furthermore, you would need to be able to offer price ranges based on these attributes. For example, the older a tree gets the more valuable it would become so you could have a range of age options presented to the buyer with their corresponding prices.

For Contechst Books, the matter is slightly different. The type of attributes we are really concerned about are things like whether the cover is soft or hardback, whether the book comes with an accompanying CD, whether it is downloadable, or whether it has more than one edition. Obviously, you will need to understand the range of options inherent in your specific selection of stock before working on this section.

Once you have a list of all the attributes that could have more than one value, you should enter meaningful names into the first group of textboxes under the heading Product Options on the Products Attributes page as shown here:

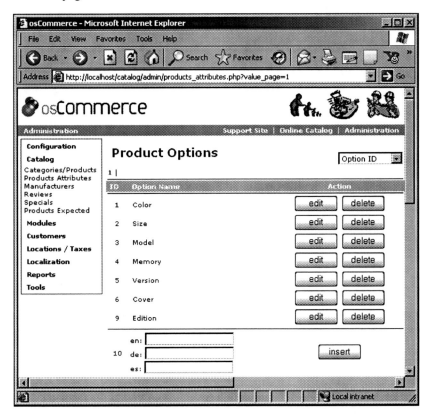

From this it is quite clear that we have added options 6 and 9, which will apply to some, if not all, of the books we are selling. Remember that the attributes you set in this section don't have to apply to a wide range of products; even if there is a single product that comes in a variety of flavors, you will need to add the attribute here in order to have the options presented to the buyer. You may recall that we also talked about whether a book would be downloadable; well, this attribute falls neatly under the Version title, so we have not added a new Product Option for downloads.

> Due to the way in which osCommerce and the download controller community contribution works, it is recommended that you look at the *Working with Downloadable Products* section of Chapter 7 before attempting to set up a working downloadable-product site.

One you have your options safely entered, move across the screen to the Option Values section. This section deals with the specifics of each of the options declared in the first section. So, for example, we would define two values for Cover here, namely Hardback and Paperback. The following screenshot shows the rest of the settings used for the demo site's products:

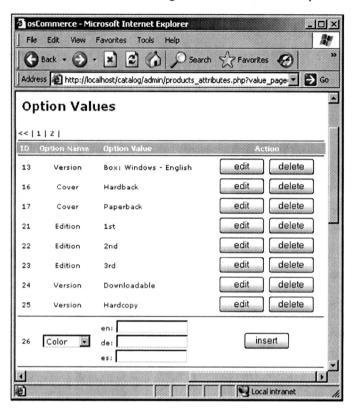

Make sure you can do this yourself by first selecting an option to work on from the drop-down list (shown in the screenshot above as ID number 26) under Option Values, then add the option value to the text box and click insert.

Now, should the issue arise, we would be able to provide a user with the options of purchasing either the Hardback or Paperback covers (if a book comes in both), or the 1st, 2nd, or 3rd edition of the book (obviously if there is only one edition of a book you simply don't associate this attribute with that book), and finally if there is a Downloadable version as well as a paper version of a book, then customers can decide which they prefer.

The final stage is to actually tie these settings to the relevant title. So, say for example, the VirtualDub book we talked about earlier had two editions as well as being bound in both hardback and paperback. We would need to ensure that the buyers could stipulate their preference while making purchases. In order to do this you scroll down to the final section, which is entitled Product Attributes as shown here:

Products Attributes

<< | 1 | 2 |

ID	Product Name	Option Name	Option Value	Value Price	Prefix	Action	
10	Microsoft IntelliMouse Explorer	Model	PS/2	0.0000	+	edit	delete
32	Unreal Tournament	Color	16 mb	0.0000	+	edit	delete
26	Unreal Tournament	Version	Download: Windows - English	0.0000	+	edit	delete
27	Unreal Tournament	Version	Box: Windows - English	0.0000	+	edit	delete
35	VirtualDub Video: Capture, Processing and Encoding	Cover	Hardback	4.0000	+	edit	delete
37	VirtualDub Video: Capture, Processing and Encoding	Edition	1st	0.0000		edit	delete
34	VirtualDub Video: Capture, Processing and Encoding	Edition	2nd	5.0000	+	edit	delete
38	VirtualDub Video: Capture, Processing and Encoding	Cover	Paperback	0.0000		edit	delete
39	VirtualDub Video: Capture, Processing and Encoding	Version	Downloadable	7.00	-	insert	

Filename: [   ] Expiry days: [7] Maximum download count: [5]

At the bottom of the table you are presented with a drop-down list of all your products as well as the product options, values, and resulting modification to the price. This is really where you get down to business and associate the attributes with their respective products. As you can see in the above figure, the VirtualDub title has had two Edition options added, with 1st and 2nd as their values, as well as Hardback and Paperback Cover options too.

The Value Price column heading holds the value of the change to the standard price, and the Prefix column shows whether or not this change is positive or negative. If you leave out these values when adding a product attribute, then osCommerce defaults to no change in price. You should be able to tell that in this case, the Hardback version will cost $4 more than a normal book, and the second edition is $5 more expensive than the first edition. Notice that the Downloadable Version of the book (the Product Attribute in the process of being added) is actually $7 cheaper than its standard counterpart.

The upshot of all this is that when a customer decides to buy a copy of VirtualDub, they have a series of choices that affect the type of product they purchase. In this case, let's say the customer wanted a first edition hardcopy, hardback version of the book. Well, in this case, they would make the selections as shown below:

And the total price would, as we expect, be $29.99 plus $4.00, which it duly is when we view the cart contents:

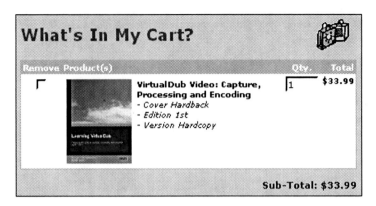

Notice that the actual options specified when the choice is originally made are now displayed underneath the product's name. The price is $33.99 as we expected, but had we bought the downloadable version it would have been $7.00 cheaper. Many of you should be frowning at this stage because *something just isn't right*! What could it be?

I must confess that you have been led astray slightly in order to demonstrate the need to plan ahead. Adding attributes such as the ones we have shown here will lead to inconsistent charges because we have failed to carefully identify the nature of each option. Obviously, if we categorize related attributes differently we can set up inconsistencies in the way the products present their options. In this case, we should not be able to choose a downloadable hardback book because it is *impossible* to have such a thing.

So where did we go wrong? The answer is quite simple! The hardback, softback, and downloadable product attributes are related in that they specify the type, or version, of book we are offering. Sure, the first two are a type of cover as well, but this is why it can be tricky to just jump in and make decisions like this. In order to rectify this problem we need to realize that a book cannot be a combination of hardback, softback, and downloadable, while it can be a combination of softback and edition one or two, hardback and edition one or two, or downloadable and edition one or two.

Accordingly, the solution is to go back and remove the category Cover, and insert Hardback and Paperback into the Version option, so buyers have to pick one of the three, but no more. Of course, trying to delete Cover will result in the following message from osCommerce:

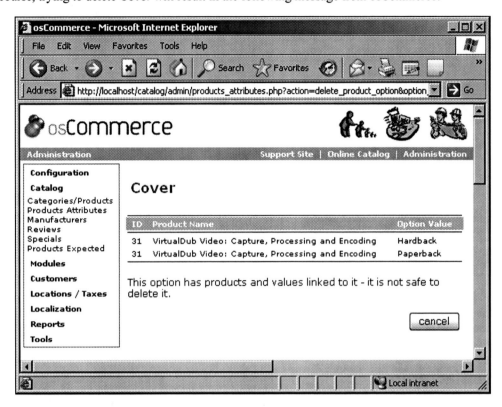

osCommerce quite rightly forces us to think carefully about what we are removing in order to maintain a valid and accurate list of product attributes at all times. This means we have to remove the settings from the Product Attributes section first, followed by the Option Values section before finally removing the Cover attribute entirely. Once this is done, the two cover options can be added to the Version attribute and associated with the book again. Now when the customer attempts to purchase the book, they are presented with *sensible* options, like so:

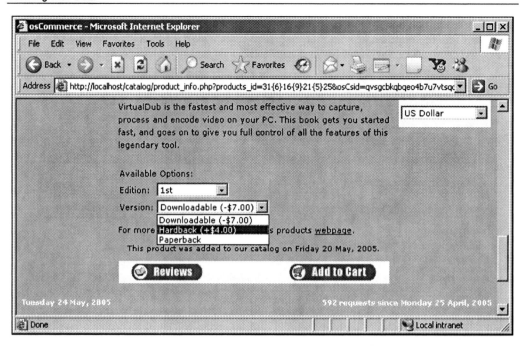

One thing to note before we move on is that it can be quite a pest to perform a large number of operations one at a time using this interface, so careful planning and using the drop-down list (at the top center of the screen) to toggle between listing the attributes by ID or alphabetically will help keep frustration to a minimum.

Manufacturers

The Manufacturers section is pretty straightforward. Using this section is a case of adding or removing the names and logos of the companies who make your products. Recall that the manufacturers declared in this section play a role in adding a product to the database since one of the drop-down lists available in that section links the manufacturers to the product. Apart from this, it is easy to add a manufacturer; simply click on insert and type in the name of the manufacturer, add a link to the location of the logo image, which will be held somewhere in your images folder, and then insert the URLs for the company's site(s), like so:

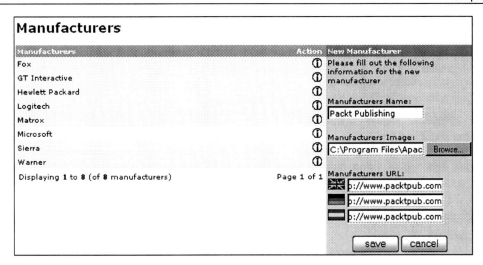

Clicking on save should bring up a screen similar to the following one. (Note that if you are not dealing with images yet, instead of the nice green message along the top of the screen there will be an alarming pink one with a warning that no file was uploaded.)

Of course, it is no problem if you want to come back at a later stage and edit your manufacturers. Simply clicking on edit will bring up the same screen as the insert button, which will allow you to change whatever you need to. Recall that in the case of the demo site, the manufacturers are in fact publishers and we are going to modify the site to reflect this in the next chapter. Doing this will serve as a nice example of how to get your hands dirty by making modifications directly to the PHP files that make up osCommerce's customer interface.

Finally, there are a few options that you should consider closely while deleting a manufacturer. The first is whether or not to delete the manufacturer's image, and the second is whether or not to remove all trace of the manufacturer's products including reviews, specials, and upcoming products. How you decide on these is really up to you, but unless you have a major fallout with the sales rep for a particular company, it is unlikely you will need to use this option that often.

Reviews

As with all good websites, the administrator has the final say on what reviews actually remain on the site. So when rival companies begin writing reviews like "*So and so's products are designed by baboons*" all over your site, you have the ability to delete or edit these reviews appropriately. Remember that reviews will be added by customers on the website, so this facility should really only be used for a moderator-type role. It is easy enough to click on edit and insert text or modify the star rating, or delete a review by clicking on delete, so we won't discuss this any further here.

Specials

At some stage you will no doubt want to offer specials to boost sales or clear old stock. Whatever your reasons, this section makes it easy to add whatever products you want to the specials list and specify how long they are to remain on special offer and how much to take off (either a set amount or a percentage), like so:

Like so many other things in the administration tool, you can, of course, edit and delete specials with ease. The upshot of adding a special, however, is that predictably, every once in a while (depending on how many products you have on special), your new product will pop up in the specials box as well as displaying its new price in a different color like so:

One final thing to note is that you can activate or deactivate any specials by using the pink and green buttons on the specials homepage.

Products Expected

At first glance, this section might seem slightly superfluous because it is easy enough to set when a product is in or out of stock and when it is expected to arrive from the Categories/Products section, which we looked at earlier in the chapter in the *Preparing to Add Product Data* section. Actually, its function is exactly the same as the adding a product page; it simply provides an interface to show all the expected products in one place. Useful if you have several hundred products coming in at any one time!

When a new product is entered into the catalog, it is not necessary for that product to physically be present at your place of work yet. Accordingly, you can set a date from the pop-up calendar that stipulates when the product is expected to arrive. Provided the product has an arrival date in the future, the product will appear in the Products Expected page. There is only one option given for the products in the Products Expected page, and that is edit.

Clicking on edit simply brings up the same page used to add the product to the database in the first place, and from here you can make any necessary changes. For example, if your product has arrived early, you can set the date expected to the current date and the product will no longer be listed in the Products Expected page. Anything with an expected date prior to the current date will not show up on this list.

Apart from making life easy when trying to keep track of when all your expected products are to arrive, setting expected arrival dates will also cause osCommerce to inform customers of the expected date on the actual site, with notes, for example, such as this one:

This product will be in stock on Thursday 26 May, 2006.

As well as this, upcoming products are displayed at the bottom of the index page on the site along with their expected date.

Customers

The Customers section provides a tool that can be used to search for registered customers by name, view and edit their details, check their orders, delete them from the database, and email them if necessary. By and large most of this information is taken care of by the site; the customers can register their details themselves and can keep them updated as and when necessary from the account page provided for all customers by osCommerce. The following figure shows the default customer account page from which customers can look after their details:

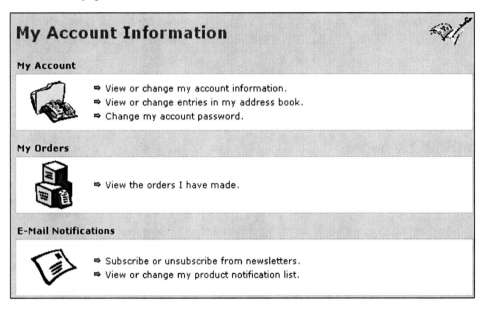

This is effectively the same functionality that the administration tool offers you as the administrator. For example, if you click on edit you are shown all the users' details in pretty much the same manner as they see them on the website. The only interesting bit of information that you may find useful here is that if you are using a fresh installation of osCommerce, and your user, or the default user, has not placed any orders on the system, then clicking on order might bring up the following page:

Orders

Order ID: [   ]
Status: [All Orders ▾]

1064 - You have an error in your SQL syntax; check the manual that corresponds to your MySQL server version for the right syntax to use near '-20, 20' at line 1

select o.orders_id, o.customers_name, o.customers_id, o.payment_method, o.date_purchased, o.last_modified, o.currency, o.currency_value, s.orders_status_name, ot.text as order_total from orders o left join orders_total ot on (o.orders_id = ot.orders_id), orders_status s where o.customers_id = '3' and o.orders_status = s.orders_status_id and s.language_id = '1' and ot.class = 'ot_total' order by orders_id DESC limit -20, 20

[TEP STOP]

While this is certainly a hideous message to behold, it is nothing particularly serious and certainly nothing to give up the whole thing and go home over. It's a bit of a bug in the system in that there is no nice, user-friendly message telling you that no orders have been placed yet. As soon as you log onto your site, and place a dummy order, this message will disappear and you will be shown the order.

You should note that if you wish to delete a customer from your database for some reason, you may want to delete the orders associated with that customer first (assuming you don't want them to remain on the system) because otherwise you will be left with a bunch of customer-less orders floating around—at least, these orders will be inaccessible from the Customers section. Of course, it is often useful to keep all the orders on your system regardless, for sales figures and so on.

Orders

A working Orders page provides quite a lot of functionality, and looks like the following screenshot. Notice that there is no option to search through the orders according to the customer's name. This is because you can view all the orders of a particular customer by pressing the orders button in the Customers section—in this way both searches by name and order ID are provided:

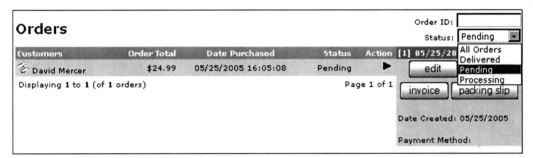

There is a drop-down list that provides a filter for which results are to be displayed depending on the status of the order. It is more than likely that you will use this or the Order ID text box to cut down the size of your results since the number of orders will grow (hopefully) quite large with time. These two options provide a particularly good way of finding otherwise well-hidden orders, especially if you need to perform some form of manual processing.

There are four options for dealing with a specific order once it has been located. These include edit, delete, invoice, and packing slip. Of these, edit is by far the most interesting, so let's look at that first. On the edit page, you are presented with the order's relevant details such as the customer's address, email address, shipping and billing address, and payment method. The actual products purchased are also shown followed by information on the status of the order, as shown here:

Customer:	David Mercer 31 Hamilton Rd Claremont Cape Town, 7708 WP, South Africa	Shipping Address:	Billing Address:	David Mercer 31 Hamilton Rd Claremont Cape Town, 7708 WP, South Africa

Telephone Number: 021 671 6700
E-Mail Address: davidm@contechst.com

Payment Method:

Products	Model	Tax	Price (ex)	Price (inc)	Total (ex)	Total (inc)
1 x VirtualDub Video: Capture, Processing and Encoding - *Edition: 2nd (+$5.00)* - *Version: Downloadable (-$7.00)*	VirtualDub	0%	$24.99	$24.99	$24.99	$24.99

Sub-Total: **$24.99**
Total: **$24.99**

Date Added	Customer Notified	Status	Comments
05/25/2005 16:05:09	✓	Pending	

Comments

```
[                                    ]
```

Status: [Pending ▼]   [update]
Notify Customer: ☑ Append Comments: ☑

[invoice] [packing slip] [back]

The important bit comes right at the bottom of the screen where you are given a text area to enter some comments, a drop-down list to change the status of the order, and a checkbox to notify the customer of any changes in the Status of the order, as well as one to Append Comments to the order. Being able to change the status of an order manually is critical for those shops that accept payments by check or in some other form that is not easily automated, and being able to add comments is important if you wish to keep a customer updated about the state of his or her purchase.

The invoice and packing slip options simply pull up a new page with invoice or packing slip details that you can print out and use if you so wish. Please be aware that both, the invoice, and packing slip have the osCommerce logo on them and you will obviously want to replace this when you have created your own site's logo. We will leave this for now since we haven't dealt with images yet, but remember to do this at some stage before invoicing customers; all you need to do is open up the invoice.php and packingslip.php files and find the line which reads something like this:

```
tep_image(DIR_WS_IMAGES . 'oscommerce.gif', 'osCommerce', '204', '50');
```

Replace this with something more suitable:

```
tep_image(DIR_WS_IMAGES . 'contechst_books.gif', 'Contechst Books', '375',
'50');
```

In this case, the image folder in question is actually the `images` folder contained in the `admin` folder and not the main `images` folder in the `catalog` directory. Make sure you place your GIF file in the right place otherwise you will end up with a broken link.

Finally, the delete command gets rid of the specified order, and rather usefully, enquires as to whether or not you would like to re-add the stock associated with the order back to your store's stock. This is, of course, very useful if, for example, a customer's credit card has proved invalid.

Viewing Reports

The reports section provides a nice method of ascertaining which products are viewed the most often, which products are the most popular by sales, and which customers are the biggest spenders—certainly all useful information for the conscientious business owner. Obviously this information can be of vital importance while determining how to order new stock or working out which demographics are the biggest spenders in your store—possibly for creating targeted promotions and so on.

Actually viewing the reports is basic stuff so we need not cover it in too much depth here, other than to say that the information provided here is only a fraction of the information that is actually saved by your system and, of course, the layout of the data doesn't come with colorful graphs and so on. If you are looking to capture more or different types of info, as well as have access to different methods of presenting the data, then the community contributions are the way to go. In fact, in Chapter 7 we will look at how to generate custom reports for low stock levels. You might find that you need a variety of different reports, so going over this example will set you up to add whatever reports you like in future.

Summary

Designing and implementing your product data structure is one of the most vital jobs involved in setting up your osCommerce store and hopefully you now find it quite easy. You should feel pretty relaxed at this stage because you have almost all your data-related needs sorted out, or at the very least, understand exactly *how to* deal with your data.

From this chapter, you have learned that categorizing your products and setting their attributes is not quite as straightforward as it may seem on the surface. Provided you think before you act, you will be just fine with regards to sorting out which attributes apply to which products. Of course, dealing with data can be fairly tricky even if you have a good structure, and we have seen how osCommerce helps us handle data updates and changes by giving us various options such as linking or duplicating, or warning us if we are trying to delete something with dependencies.

With that said, it is time to give our site a full facelift and nose job. The next chapter talks about customization, and it is here that we will finally discuss how to properly deal with the images you want to put up on your site.

5
Customization

I will grant that up 'til now, the site as shown in many of the screenshots looks pretty mangy, with a gray body area, broken image links, box headings that don't match the background, default text that means nothing in the context of the new site, and so forth. All of this needs to be changed to a professional and aesthetically pleasing interface, which will help encourage and facilitate the purchase of your goods.

Sounds easy enough, doesn't it? Well, in a way it is and in a way it isn't. The reason we still have designers with jobs is because by and large the average person on the street finds it difficult to produce a site that looks like it has had money invested in the design. But as much as they would tell you differently, designers (or *creatives* as I believe they are called) aren't mythically endowed with superhuman senses to help them decide what does look good and what doesn't. Anyone can do it, to varying degrees, by following the usual *think before you act* paradigm and applying a *process* to how they go about the business of designing a site.

Playing around with different combinations of color and layout is always worthwhile, and often teaches you more about the best way to do things than any process or book. You also have the luxury of having a website set up for you, which frees you to simply make changes here and there to achieve your design goals rather than develop the HTML from scratch. To some extent, this luxury actually restricts you because anything short of a total rewrite of the pages will mean your site retains some of the osCommerce *flavor*. But that's not a bad thing at all!

In this chapter, we will look at the following topics:

- Language definitions
- Working with boxes and columns
- Dealing with images
- Modifying the stylesheet
- A few miscellaneous customizations

I should warn you before we continue that there is quite a lot involved with coming up with an entirely fresh, pleasing, and distinct look to a site. There are lots of fiddly little bits to play around with, so you should be prepared to spend a bit of time on this section because, after all, your site's look and feel is really the face of your business.

Another thing to remember before we begin is that you should take some time to look at what is already out there. Many issues that you will encounter while designing your site have already been successfully dealt with all over the show—not only by osCommerce users of course. Also, don't be scared to treat your design as an ongoing process—while it is never good to drastically change your site on a weekly basis, regular tweaking or upgrading of your interface can keep it modern and looking shiny new.

Language Definitions

Obviously, there are quite a lot of modifications that need to be made to the default language in osCommerce. You may or may not want to change the headings of boxes, error messages, page text, and pretty much anything else that involves language on the site. In order to do this you need to edit the language of the various files presented in the Define Language section under Tools in the administration section. Navigating to this will bring up a screen with a host of different files available for editing (note that you can also do this through the File Manager section, but this will expose all the code in the file to you, which may well make it harder to do a simple language edit):

Define Language

english.php	account.php
account_edit.php	account_history.php
account_history_info.php	account_newsletters.php
account_notifications.php	account_password.php
address_book.php	address_book_process.php
advanced_search.php	checkout_confirmation.php
checkout_payment.php	checkout_payment_address.php
checkout_process.php	checkout_shipping.php
checkout_shipping_address.php	checkout_success.php
conditions.php	contact_us.php
cookie_usage.php	create_account.php
create_account_success.php	download.php
index.php	info_shopping_cart.php
login.php	logoff.php
password_forgotten.php	privacy.php
products_new.php	product_info.php
product_reviews.php	product_reviews_info.php
product_reviews_write.php	reviews.php
shipping.php	shopping_cart.php
specials.php	ssl_check.php
tell_a_friend.php	

You can choose which language you want to work on by selecting it from the drop-down list at the top right of the screen. Please note that we will only deal with English in this book, since all the principles that apply to *one* language apply to *any* language. Also, Contechst Books only publishes English-language books, so it makes sense to only have the website in English.

Now, as you might have guessed, your job is to now go through each and every one of the files to modify the site to suit your needs. Editing a file is very simple: simply click on the name of the file and make the appropriate changes directly to the text. Let's take a look at some of the more important files in this section by way of example.

english.php

Recall that Contechst Books does not have manufacturers, but would rather use the term 'publisher' on the site. Well, in order to make these changes, we open up english.php and change the occurrences of Manufacturer to Publisher, as shown in the following screenshot:

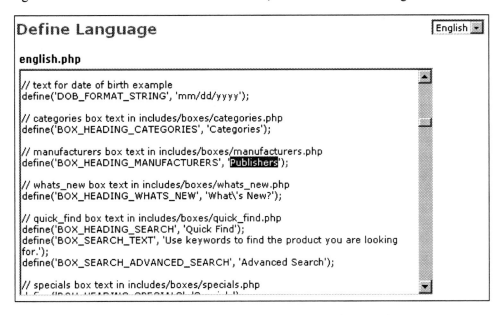

The highlighted text shows where the term Manufacturers has been changed to Publishers. Can you guess what effect this change will have on the site? Well, if you look at the line immediately above the one that was changed, which is a PHP comment line, you will see that this setting affects the includes/boxes/manufacturers.php file. This is because the english.php file actually holds information on all the generic language used on the site. Looking at it from another point of view, all expressions used only once, by one special file, should be or are in *their appropriate file*, and all other expressions that are used several times are in english.php.

As well as this, bear in mind that each file in the catalog folder has its partner file in the includes/languages/english folder to define the language terms there. Accordingly, rather than using the editor that is provided by osCommerce, you might want to open up the english.php file (or any other language file, for that matter) in a nice editor such as EditPlus in order to make it easier for you to edit the file. We will show the files being used from the admin tool for demonstrative purposes, but you will probably find you prefer to use a proper editor.

Now, look at the `define` statement again. It declares that the `BOX_HEADING_MANUFACTURERS` constant, which is used in the `includes/boxes/manufacturers.php` file, is the word Publishers. From this you should suspect that the heading of the manufacturers' box, which is shown on all the pages of the site, will now be Publishers instead of Manufacturers. Taking a quick glance at the site confirms this (look at the box on the bottom left):

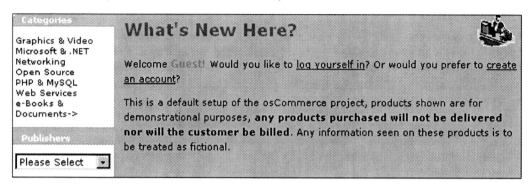

This, of course, is not the only occurrence of the term Manufacturer on the site! There are other candidates to replace, so we can continue searching our `english.php` file for the term Manufacturer. Before we do, though, make note of one very important point:

> These are PHP statements, which you are modifying, so you need to be aware that any changes to the actual code, such as removing a semi-colon by accident or adding in a single quote without escaping it with a backslash, will result in problems.

Take a look at the setting below the one we changed in the earlier screenshot to see an example of how a backslash escapes a quote in the text part of a `define` statement. As it so happens, we need only make one more replacement of the term Manufacturer, as well as converting this line:

```
define('HEADER_TITLE_MY_ACCOUNT', 'My Account');
```

to this line:

```
define('HEADER_TITLE_MY_ACCOUNT', 'Your Account');
```

and we are done with this file for now (the last change rewords the account login presented at the top right of the screen simply because I prefer this wording). Before we move on, though, it is useful to make note of the main files and parts of the site covered by `english.php`:

- `header.php`
- `footer.php`
- Box text
- Error messages
- Customer-information text
- Navigation text

- Image button text

- Personalized greeting text

- Footer text—you will probably want to remove this or change it to your own copyright notice. (Please read the conditions for modifying this text, given in the comment above it in the english.php file.)

Remember to always check that whatever changes you make to these files don't cause errors or unexpected results on the site. Apart from that, you simply need to implement whichever changes you require as you go along. Most of the default text is pretty standard and shouldn't need too much attention.

index.php

When you first log on to your osCommerce site, the index page provides you with lots of helpful information about how to do things and where to go for help. This obviously needs a complete overhaul, and specifically in the case of the demo site, we don't want to waste readers' time with a whole lot of information. Since we are a specialist bookstore, we expect the customer who is visiting to be looking specifically for technical books, so rather than introduce ourselves and tell them what we do (because they more than likely know), we want to display our newest and upcoming products.

Accordingly, the first change we make to the file is change the first line of code to the following:

```
define('TEXT_MAIN', '');
```

Now remember: this may not be necessarily suitable for your store! You may wish to add some introductory information, especially if you are retailing a product that merits a bit of explanation. If this is the case, create your text based on the guidelines of good language design (there is a discussion on Search Engine Optimization in the final chapter) and insert it in between the empty quotes in the TEXT_MAIN define statement. Remember to add HTML tags where appropriate to emphasize important points and so forth, as well as escape any single quote characters with a backslash.

Apart from this change, we have also had to replace a few occurrences of Manufacturer, with Publisher on the following lines:

```
define('TABLE_HEADING_MANUFACTURER', 'Publisher');
define('TEXT_ALL_MANUFACTURERS', 'All Publishers');
```

Again, since we don't wish to have the chirpy Let's see what we have here text at the top of our product category pages, the relevant line was changed to this:

```
define('HEADING_TITLE', '');
```

Please bear in mind that while this means that no text will be shown because of the empty string provided in the HEADING_TITLE define statement, it doesn't mean that the space allotted to this text disappears. If you want to remove this space completely, then you need to work with the HTML that is responsible for this section of the page directly.

A category page, in this case PHP & MySQL, after these modifications looks like this:

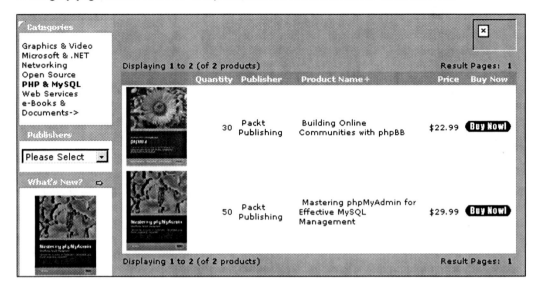

Notice that the box heading in the category listing now reads Publisher instead of Manufacturer, and that the usual Let's see what we have here text is absent. Of course, we still have a horrid broken link at the top right of the screen, but this will be dealt with in the *Dealing with Images* section later in this chapter.

The rest of the files by and large deal with cosmetic touches and will not really impact on the running of your site barring one or two exceptions. For example, you will need to insert your own information into the conditions.php and privacy.php files in order to present accurate legal information about your store.

Incidentally, when you look at a product listing such as the one shown in the previous screenshot, you will notice that there is a plus sign next to the Product Name column heading. This is because, along with the other headings in the product listing, you can order the results in ascending or descending form. I leave it to you to play around with this to get the hang of it—if you don't think that this functionality is obvious, then perhaps you could do something to ensure that your customers know it exists. A note about it on the page, or highlighting the links might work in this case.

Using HTML for Language Formatting

Since we are on the topic of language, there is a useful little trick that you may as well learn here since these two files (conditions.php and privacy.php) are closely related. Often on the 'conditions' and 'terms of use page' of a site, there is a heading called 'privacy', with a link to a page that holds all the privacy information. This happens because, intuitively, the privacy conditions should come under the conditions heading, but there is often too much information to present on a single page and anyway it helps to distinguish the two logically. Accordingly you will need to know how to create a link from one page to the other.

The conditions and terms of use page on `contechst.com` uses a link to take the reader to the privacy page within the actual body of the text. This is accomplished using the HTML `<a>` tag, with an `href` attribute. The actual line in the text looks like this:

```
<a href=\'http://localhost/catalog/privacy.php\'>here.</a>
```

This tells the browser to render the word `here` as a link, which the user can click on to open up the page specified by the `href` attribute—in this case `http://localhost/catalog/privacy.php`. Notice that the single quotes that are used to delimit the URL have to be escaped with a backslash for the benefit of osCommerce.

> **Important**: While the method shown here is pretty standard, you might want to consider the fact that it is possible that this will not propagate your customer's session ID. Make sure you check that sessions are maintained. If they aren't, then you will need to use the `tep_href_link` function like so:
> ```
> <a href="'.tep_href_link(FILENAME_PRIVACY, '', 'NONSSL').'">'.'here'.'</a>.
> ```

So, we can now go from the `conditions.php` file as shown here (at present the formatting for the link is similar to the background color, so the here part of the sentence under Privacy doesn't show up well):

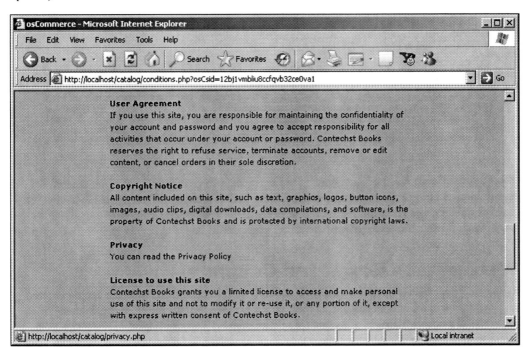

to the privacy policy page, `privacy.php`, which is shown here:

Privacy Notice

Use of your Personal Information
We use your personal information for the following purposes:

- To deliver goods to you that you ordered directly from us
- To deliver electronic services, such as newsletters or downloads that you request
- To help us create and publish content most relevant to you.
- To alert you to amendments, corrections, special offers, updated information and other new services from Contechst Books, if you so request.
- To allow you access to limited-entry areas of our site as appropriate.

Notice that quite a lot of formatting has been done to this text using HTML. The only way you will learn how to achieve the language formatting you desire is by practicing and practicing. As a matter of interest, the HTML for the section of the Privacy Notice that is visible in the previous screenshot, is shown here:

```
<b>Use of your Personal Information</b>
<br />
We use your personal information for the following purposes:
<br />
<br />
<ul>
  <li>To deliver goods to you that you ordered directly from us  </li>
  <li>To deliver electronic services, such as newsletters or downloads that
you request  </li>
  <li>To help us create and publish content most relevant to you.  </li>
  <li>To alert you to amendments, corrections, special offers, updated
information and other new services from Contechst Books, if you so request.
</li>
  <li>To allow you access to limited-entry areas of our site as appropriate.
</li>
</ul>
```

Specifically, the bulleted list is achieved by using the `<ul>` tag, which renders an unordered list, and its corresponding bullet points are created using the `<li>` tag, which stands for list item. We don't have time to go into a full-on tutorial on HTML, but you are certainly encouraged to play around with it enough to become proficient.

Working with Boxes and Columns

As you will have noticed over the course of the book so far, the site consists of a central column reserved for text or product images and information, surrounded on either side by columns of boxes, which hold anything from the navigation structure to a keyword search. Naturally, you might wish to change this general structure in favor of something that suits your site better. There is really an unlimited number of possible changes, and you could quite easily alter the structure sufficiently to eradicate most if not all the evidence of the original layout.

For the first time, we are going to put down the administration tool and get involved directly with the PHP code within the site's files, and to get the ball rolling, we will start by removing a box. You know by now that `contechst.com` retails only English-language books and so there is now no longer any need to have a box showing the various languages available on the site. As a result, we would like to erase this box from the right-hand column entirely because it no longer serves any function. This is about the simplest operation we can perform on the site; it involves commenting out only a single line per box removed.

Removing a Box

Go to the `includes/column_right.php` file in your `catalog` folder and open it up using your favorite editor. This file is responsible for including all the boxes found in the right-hand column of the site's web pages. Now, look around the file until you find the following lines:

```
if (substr(basename($PHP_SELF), 0, 8) != 'checkout') {
    include(DIR_WS_BOXES . 'languages.php');
    include(DIR_WS_BOXES . 'currencies.php');
}
```

What do you think this statement is saying? Well, if you look at the first line involving an `if` statement, you can read it to mean:

If the substring of the `$PHP_SELF` variable—that holds the pagename of the current page—from the first character to the ninth, is not equal to the `checkout` string, then include the two files written here.

This is because, by default, the only time that you don't want the customer to be able to change the language of the page is when you are already checking out any purchases he or she has made. At all other times, the languages box is displayed. Now, because we want to modify this behavior to never show the languages box, we simply want to prevent PHP from reading the `include` statement that inserts the box. We can do this with a simple comment, which will modify the statement to the following:

```
if (substr(basename($PHP_SELF), 0, 8) != 'checkout') {
    // include(DIR_WS_BOXES . 'languages.php');
    include(DIR_WS_BOXES . 'currencies.php');
}
```

Now, as always, we need to save these changes and go to the site to ensure that the modification has had the expected results. Looking at an arbitrary page that is not part of the checkout-process page (because the box is never displayed here anyway), we can see that the languages box is no longer shown down the right-hand side:

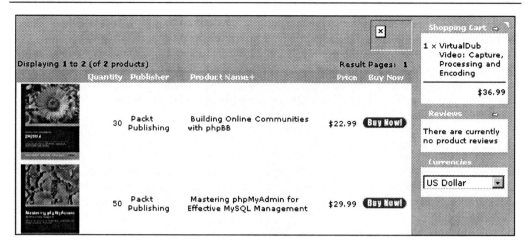

The process is really the same for removing any other box on the site. But what happens if you now want to move a box so that it appears before any other box—or even move it to the other column?

Moving Boxes

To move a box around, you simply have to move the statement that includes the box in the code. If you wanted to change columns, then you would have to move the code statement to the relevant column file—either the column_left.php or column_right.php file, depending on whether you wanted it on the left or right.

For example, let's say you want to move Currencies to appear above the Reviews box in the right-hand column. Copy and cut the following statement (which we have already seen):

```
if (substr(basename($PHP_SELF), 0, 8) != 'checkout') {
    // include(DIR_WS_BOXES . 'languages.php');
    include(DIR_WS_BOXES . 'currencies.php');
}
```

and paste it as shown here in the same file:

```
if (isset($HTTP_GET_VARS['products_id'])) {
    if (basename($PHP_SELF) != FILENAME_TELL_A_FRIEND) include(DIR_WS_BOXES .
'tell_a_friend.php');
} else {
    include(DIR_WS_BOXES . 'specials.php');
}

if (substr(basename($PHP_SELF), 0, 8) != 'checkout') {
    // include(DIR_WS_BOXES . 'languages.php');
    include(DIR_WS_BOXES . 'currencies.php');
}

    require(DIR_WS_BOXES . 'reviews.php');
```

Save the changes, and view the results in an arbitrary file, once again avoiding the checkout pages. You will notice that the boxes have swapped around as intended:

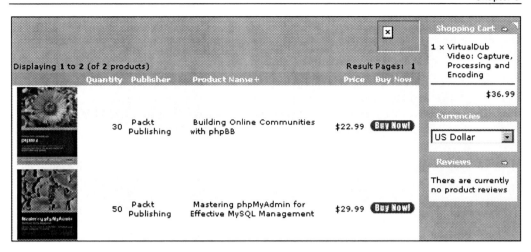

It will be left to the reader to swap boxes between the left and right columns as desired. However, this should really only be an exercise because the left-hand side is already well organized as part of a tool to help customers locate the products they are searching for. What would be really nice now is if we could add a short note to the Currencies box to explain to customers that the exchange rate is not a live exchange rate, but has a lag of, say, up to two days.

Modifying Box Content

There are a couple of ways to go about modifying boxes, and one is more correct that the other. "What could he possibly be on about, saying that one method is *more* correct than the other?" you may ask. Surely if both work then both are equally correct! This is perfectly true, but when I refer to degrees of correctness, what I mean is that the designers of osCommerce have gone about building the site in specific way, and if you modify the code in your site, you should at all times try to maintain the same conventions as the original site. If you don't, it will be nearly impossible to *guess* how you made certain alterations when you come back to them in a year or so.

Sticking to the same conventions used by the osCommerce team will keep your code neat and easy to follow for anyone who has to look over it in the future. However, depending on what it is you need to do, it may not be possible to always stick to the coding convention. Because of this, I will show two methods of changing the Currencies box to insert a little note above the drop-down list of currencies—one involving the direct manipulation of code in the box file, and the other using osCommerce's in-place convention.

The first method is more straightforward and is easier to implement. However, the second is the more *correct* method and is the one that is recommended.

Open up the code file that is responsible for creating the Currencies box, `includes/boxes/currencies.php`. Look for the code that is used for populating the box's content. It looks like this:

```
$info_box_contents[] = array('form' => tep_draw_form('currencies',
tep_href_link(basename($PHP_SELF), '', $request_type, false), 'get'), 'align'
=> 'center', 'text' => tep_draw_pull_down_menu('currency', $currencies_array,
$currency, 'onChange="this.form.submit();" style="width: 100%"') .
$hidden_get_variables . tep_hide_session_id());
```

Don't worry about understanding everything here—it's not important or relevant to you at the moment. What is important is that you can see that we have a variable called $info_box_contents, which is being filled with the information given on the right of the assignment (=) operator. From the name you should be able to deduce that this is the variable that will contain the contents of the Currencies information box.

Now, we want to add the note above the drop-down list, so we append it to the front of the text contents with the . operator and enclose it in quotes to denote that it is a string, like so:

```
$info_box_contents[] = array('form' => tep_draw_form('currencies',
tep_href_link(basename($PHP_SELF), '', $request_type, false), 'get'), 'align'
=> 'center', 'text' => 'NOTE: Prices given in any currency other than US
dollars are calculated from an exchange rate which is determined weekly. <br>'
. tep_draw_pull_down_menu('currency', $currencies_array, $currency,
'onChange="this.form.submit();" style="width: 100%"') . $hidden_get_variables
. tep_hide_session_id());
```

Checking out the results on the site show us that we have made the changes successfully, but there is a problem in that the message doesn't look neat because it is simply too long:

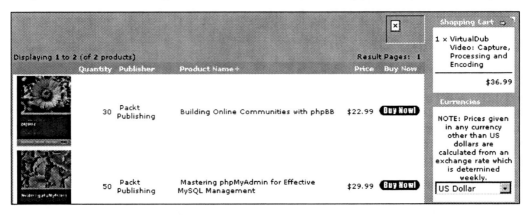

This shows that at least we can add text as we choose, but you would probably be better advised to put this type of information in your conditions.php file. However, this is fine for the purposes of this example, and so we will continue on and demonstrate the *better* way to perform this same change.

Delete any changes you have made to the box and return it to its original format. (Remember that you should really be making a backup of any files that you are worried you may break during the course of your work.) Now navigate to the Define Languages section of the admin tool and open up the english.php file discussed earlier in this chapter. Recall that one of the functions of english.php was to define a whole lot of text for various bits and pieces of the site. One of these bits is in fact the information boxes.

Navigate down to the section that deals with the Currencies box, as shown here:

```
// currencies box text in includes/boxes/currencies.php
define('BOX_HEADING_CURRENCIES', 'Currencies');
```

Now, this section is reserved for defining constants that can be used by the box files. For example, the box heading, which we know to be Currencies, is defined here. What we would like to do is follow this convention by providing a constant declaration that can be used by currencies.php to output our message to the site. Add the following line like so:

```
// currencies box text in includes/boxes/currencies.php
define('BOX_HEADING_CURRENCIES', 'Currencies');
define('BOX_CURRENCIES_TEXT', 'NOTE: Prices given in any currency other than
US dollars are calculated from an exchange rate which is determined weekly.
<br>');
```

Now go back to the currencies.php file in your editor and append the constant we have just modified to the text key of the $info_box_content variable like this:

```
$info_box_contents[] = array('form' => tep_draw_form('currencies',
tep_href_link(basename($PHP_SELF), '', $request_type, false), 'get'), 'align'
=> 'center', 'text' => BOX_CURRENCIES_TEXT .
tep_draw_pull_down_menu('currency', $currencies_array, $currency,
'onChange="this.form.submit();" style="width: 100%"') . $hidden_get_variables
. tep_hide_session_id());
```

Now when you save the changes to both files and view any of the pages that include the Currencies information box, you will see the note correctly displayed. So why is this second way more correct than the first way? Take a look over the english.php file—you will notice that all the constants used in the information boxes are defined here, so this is the logical place to add that information in the future too. Otherwise you will end up having information defined all over the show and it soon becomes quite hard to keep track of everything.

What if instead of modifying the default information boxes, we need a new box?

Adding a Box

We will demonstrate how to add a new box on our site in case you wish to add some of your own functionality at some stage. For the sake of demonstration, this box is going to be a placeholder for a live RSS feed on new technology developments that may be of interest to our customers. Don't worry if you don't know what an RSS feed is—we won't be dealing with it in this book; what is important is that you learn to add new boxes.

The new box, added to the right-hand column of the site, will be called Tech Feed, and will be based on a modified version of the currencies.php file. Make a copy of the currencies.php file in your includes/boxes folder, and call it feed.php. Then go to the column_right.php file and add this file at the bottom of the code (before the closing ?> tag), like so:

```
require(DIR_WS_BOXES . 'reviews.php');
require(DIR_WS_BOXES . 'feed.php');

?>
```

Save the file and take a look at your site. You will notice that you now have two Currencies boxes. The reason for the duplication is of course that we haven't modified feed.php to reflect the fact that it is now the Tech Feed box and not Currencies. So, to rectify this, open up feed.php in your editor and modify it so that it looks like this:

```
<!-- This is a custom box to house the contents of an RSS Feed. Originally
created on 05/30/05 -->

<tr>
  <td>
<?php
    $info_box_contents = array();
    $info_box_contents[] = array('text' => BOX_HEADING_FEED);

    new infoBoxHeading($info_box_contents, false, false);

    $info_box_contents = array();
    $info_box_contents[] = array('align' => 'center', 'text' => BOX_FEED_TEXT);

    new infoBox($info_box_contents);
?>
  </td
</tr>
```

Of course one shouldn't forget to use the english.php file to define the constants we are going to use for the feed box. So you will need to make the following additions to the english.php file—the best place to add this is directly after the code for the last box, as this is an intuitive place to look for it when you need to modify it in future:

```
// languages box text in includes/boxes/feed.php
define('BOX_HEADING_FEED', 'Tech Feed');
define('BOX_FEED_TEXT', 'This is the future site of the RSS Web Feed!');
```

Notice several things here:

The feed.php file uses the constants BOX_HEADING_FEED and BOX_FEED_TEXT, which are defined in english.php and are presented using the same convention as the rest of the files in osCommerce.

There are HTML tags before and after the PHP code in the feed.php file. This is necessary because of the way in which osCommerce handles information boxes. These tags simply tell the browser to create a new table cell within a table. The result of all this work should be much the same as the following screenshot:

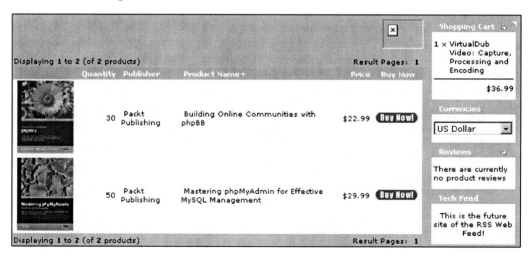

Of course, this box doesn't do anything useful yet, but as soon as you have a need for a new, out-of-the-ordinary box, you know how to add one. You can do quite a lot with boxes now, and while most of the boxes presented on the site by default are pretty useful, you now at least have the option of chopping and changing things as you see fit. Of course, we don't have to stop at modifying just boxes; we can also perform operations on the columns themselves.

Removing a Column

Working with columns is a bit of a hassle because there is no single code file that will influence the entire site. Each change you make to the columns has to be made to every page on the site. Having a column down the left-hand side of the page is generally a good idea because users are used to navigating pages from the left of the screen. Also, many sites do not have a column down the right-hand side, preferring to let their content fill the page or even show adverts down the right-hand side in any extra space.

In order to rid yourself of the right-hand column (remember you can always add any boxes you want saved to the left-hand column or any other part of the page for that matter) you will need to go to each and every page that contains the right-hand column and look for the following code:

```
<!-- right_navigation //-->
<?php
require(DIR_WS_INCLUDES . 'column_right.php');
?>
<!-- right_navigation_eof //-->
```

As you might well guess, the only change needed for removing the column entirely is to comment out that line like this:

```
<!-- right_navigation //-->
<?php
// require(DIR_WS_INCLUDES . 'column_right.php');
?>
<!-- right_navigation_eof //-->
```

This was done by way of example for the index.php file, and the results are as follows:

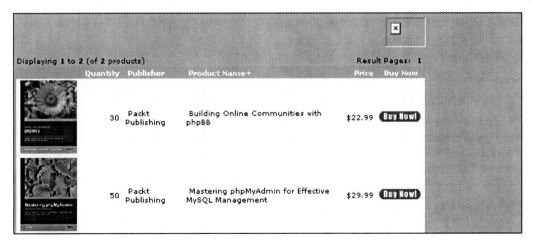

Of course, the right-hand column has disappeared, but the space it occupied has not. In order to close this space, you would need to modify the HTML on each page to remove the space allotted to this column, which should be shown directly above the column declaration. The line above the relevant column declaration reads:

```
<td width="<?php echo BOX_WIDTH; ?>" valign="top"><table border="0"
width="<?php echo BOX_WIDTH; ?>" cellspacing="0" cellpadding="2">
```

Change it to:

```
<!--
<td width="<?php echo BOX_WIDTH; ?>" valign="top"><table border="0"
width="<?php echo BOX_WIDTH; ?>" cellspacing="0" cellpadding="2">
-->
```

This will give you the following result:

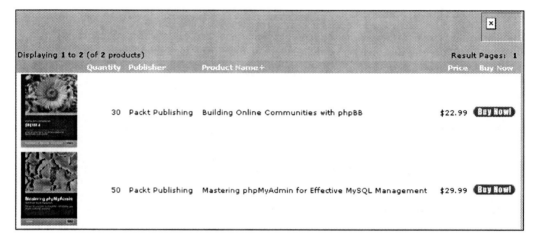

You may well want to use the space given over to the old column for something else entirely, in which case you would simply modify the require statement that calls the column_right.php file so that it calls your own file, which you have placed in the same folder as the column_right.php file. So:

```
require(DIR_WS_INCLUDES . 'column_right.php');
```

would become something like this:

```
require(DIR_WS_INCLUDES . 'custom_column.php');
```

This requires that you have created the custom_column.php file, perhaps based on the code from the original column, and that it is suitable to *fit* into the allotted space. An in-depth discussion on the page layout will come later in this chapter under the heading *Miscellaneous Customizations*. For now I am certain you will be glad that we are finally going to talk about images.

Dealing with Images

Working with images for the Web is very much an art! I don't mean this in the sense that generally you should be quite artistic in order to make nice pictures. I mean that actually managing and dealing with image files is itself an art. There is a lot of work to be done for the aspiring website owner with respect to attaining a pleasing and meaningful visual environment. This is because the Web is the one retail environment that is most reliant on visual images to have an effect on customers because sight and sound are the only two senses that are targeted by the Internet, for now.

In order to have the freedom to manipulate images as required by your site, you really need to use a reasonably powerful image editor. Photoshop or Paint Shop Pro are examples of good image editing environments, but anything that allows you to save files in a variety of different formats and provides resizing capabilities should be sufficient for a simpler looking site. Of course, if you have to take digital photographs of your products yourself, then you will need to ensure you make the photos as uniform as possible, with a background that doesn't distract from the product itself—editing the images to remove the background altogether is probably best.

There are several areas of concern when working with images, all of which need to be closely scrutinized if you hope to produce an integrated and pleasing visual shopping environment (not all of these relate to what your customers actually see, funnily enough):

- One of the biggest problems with images is that they take up a lot more memory than text or code. For this reason you need to have an effective method for dealing with large product images (or any other images) that will be required for your site—simply squashing large images into thumbnails will slow down your site because the server will still be uploading the entire, large file to the customers' machines, even if it is only showing a thumbnail on their pages.

- One common mistake people make when dealing with images is not working on them early on in the process to make them as uniform in size and type as possible. If all your images are of one size and of the same dimensions, then you are going to have things a lot easier than most. In fact, this should really be your aim before you do anything involving the site—*make sure your product images are all uniform.*

- Of course, deciding what type of image you actually want to use from the multitude available can also be a bit of an issue because some image types take up more space than others, and some may not even be rendered properly at all in a browser. By and large there are really only two image types that are most commonly used—**GIF** and **JPG**.

- The intended use of the image can also be a big factor when deciding how to create, size, and format the file. For example, icons and logos should really be saved as GIF files whereas photos and large or complex images should be saved in the JPG format.

Two types of image files were mentioned in the bulleted list. Let's take a quick look at those here:

GIF, or **Graphics Interchange Format**, is known for its compression and the fact that it can store and display multiple images. The major drawback to GIF is that images can only use up to 256 distinct colors to display their data. For photographic-quality images, this is a significant obstacle. However, you should use GIFs for:

- Images with a transparent background
- Animated graphics
- Smaller, less complex images requiring no more than 256 colors

JPG, or **JPEG (Joint Photographic Experts Group)**, should be used when presenting photo-realistic images. JPG can compress large images while retaining the overall photographic quality of the image. JPG files can use any number of colors, so it's a very convenient format for images that require a lot of colors. JPG should be used for:

- Photographs
- Larger, complex images requiring more than 256 to display properly

With that knowledge under our belts, we are now going to deal with each type of image used by Contechst Books one by one.

The images Folder

Recall that it was recommended earlier that you maintain the same conventions when altering code as the original developers of osCommerce. That lesson applies very much to images in that it is safest to keep to the same convention as the default structure when storing images and naming folders. Doing this will promote an intuitive and well-managed folder and naming structure, which will be easy to add to and modify if needs be.

Taking a look at the default images folder, you can see that there are several folders devoted to manufacturers' products, among other things, as well as a whole bunch of small GIF images. The emphasis, of course, on the GIF images is that they are small—anything more than a few KB and you are asking for speed-related problems when customers download pages:

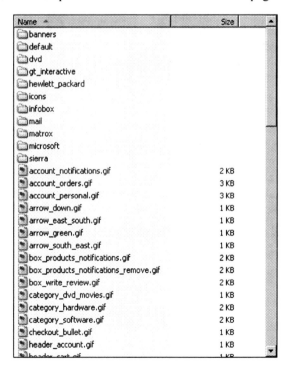

There are a few other miscellaneous folders: there's one folder (the infobox folder) for images used in the information box headings to give them a rounded feel, another folder for your banner ads (to be discussed later), and so on. The one thing to note (although it isn't visible in the screenshot opposite) is that the manufacturer images are not housed within the manufacturer's image folder, but rather directly under the main images folder—where you store these is entirely up to you, so long as your choice is consistent.

> **Warning**: By default osCommerce saves all uploaded image files to the images folder. Moving them elsewhere will break the image links unless you make some custom modifications. Holding all your images in the images folder will not affect the performance of your site in any way.

Sizing and Naming Images

Apart from where you save your images, you need to think very carefully about what you call them. The reason I say this is because you should really be aiming for a uniform, meaningful, and intuitive naming convention to make things easier should you ever have to deal with images programmatically in the future. As it just so happens, books have an obvious product-image name ready made because they all have an ISBN number that uniquely identifies them—accordingly, the demo site will use the book's ISBN number to identify the images. You should choose whatever is most appropriate for your products—so long as everything is consistently named, you should be fine.

So, now that we know where to save images and how to name them, we need to look at how big or small to make them—both in terms of size and dimensions. This is not as easy as it sounds and whether you like it or not, there is really no set formula for dealing with this. Remember that osCommerce can modify the dimensions of your thumbnail images, and these are set in the Images section of the administration tool. So, the first thing for you to do is take a look at the dimension of your thumbnail images and set the values in Images appropriately—for example, the settings in the demo site are:

Small Image Width   100

Small Image Height 125

because this suits the size of the thumbnail images being used *as well as* the purpose of the images.

Note that at this size, all the cover writing is not legible, but it is more than clear what the title is and what the cover looks like in general (see the live site at http://www.contechst.com), which is all that is needed, since customers would simply enlarge the thumbnail to get a close look at the cover. If you recall, the default settings had quite different dimensions from the ones listed here, which would distort the current images quite severely. As a result, a bit of trial and error time was spent finding the best thumbnail sizes.

Graphics—Logos and Icons

To a large extent, dealing with images that are not associated with products is a lot easier than what we have seen. You really have a few well-defined choices with regards to logos and icons, and once they are made, it is pretty straightforward to implement them. Your main concern, to begin with, is whether or not you think your site will benefit from the use of graphics or not. If yes, then you need to design a suite of your own graphics to complement the rest of the site—alternatively, of course, you can use the graphics that are supplied by default with osCommerce, but in this case you are sacrificing individuality for ease of use.

Once you have made up your mind to use graphics on your site, then the two remaining questions are *where* you will put them, and *what size* you will make them. The second question can be easily answered by fiddling around with the image settings in the admin tool to make the space allotted for icons on the site fit the dimensions of your particular graphics. The settings for the demo site are the following because they fit in nicely with the publishers' logos, and any other graphics can be made to order (in other words, you can always pick a size, and design graphics for that exact size):

Heading Image Width   65

Heading Image Height 40

The answer to the first question really relies on your sense of taste. Obviously placing functional graphics, in other words, those which possess links or perform some sort of task, is quite an important aspect because it needs to be very obvious exactly what their function is. As well as ensuring that functional graphics are placed in easily visible spots, the actual graphic should intuitively reflect its function. Take a look at the graphics provided by osCommerce to see how their designers have linked function to form. For example, they have two shopping bags:

which take customers to their cart contents page—nice and simple, but certainly intuitive!

To some extent, it is impossible to escape the use of graphics, because you will, at the very least, need a company logo of some sort, somewhere towards the top of the page to brand the site and give it some sort of identity. As well as this, there are buttons, which generally need some form of graphic in order to make them look realistic.

Contechst Books is not going to make much use of graphics above and beyond those needed for corporate branding and navigation, but by way of example, we will demonstrate how to change graphics from their defaults to the new business-specific ones (we'll cover some of the design considerations that go into this too) as well as showing how to move graphics on the page to suit your needs.

Creating and Inserting New Graphics

The demo site will obviously require a new business logo to be inserted at the top of the page. Accordingly, this section is going to concentrate on how to create and insert just such a graphic. To begin with, the original page looks like this:

We would like to create something that will fit in this space nicely and provide an elegant brand or company image, which will be displayed here instead of the osCommerce logo. So, the first thing to do is set about designing the new company image. In order to do this, we must take into account that this is a retailer of computer technology books and so it is likely that the clientele will be hard-working adult programmers or business people.

Because of this, the company image should be sophisticated and elegant, and should avoid garish or loud tones. That's not to say it can't be striking in some way, but it should not look like someone has graffitied the name onto the site. Of course, this might all sound quite boring to you, but bear in mind that your site may well have a different clientele—perhaps a marketing or advertising-based clientele that would expect a flamboyant logo.

If you are an established business, then you already know what your company logo is going to be, and you simply need to reproduce that image for insertion here. Of course, if your company already has a color scheme, then you can alter the colors presented on the site quite easily (the next section on *Modifying the Stylesheet* will cover this). Another consideration, assuming your business doesn't already have a color scheme, is that this logo will need to fit in with the site as well. But how do you know how to design your logo when the site itself hasn't been laid out?

The answer to this is, of course, that you should already have a pretty clear image of what you want your site to look like. In your head you should have the fundamental design already worked out, so you should know roughly what is required from your graphics in terms of look and feel. Now, the Contechst site, of which the bookstore demo will become a part, looks like this:

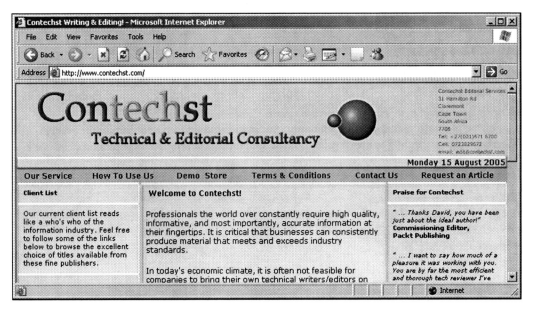

Because the store is going to become part of this site, it is obvious that we already have a rough idea of the color scheme and layout of the site. More importantly, there is a solid basis for designing the Contechst Books logo, and after no small amount of consternation the new logo is unveiled

(I decided on a slightly different color since the demo site is not directly related to parent business):

Contechst Books

Now, this still look a bit boring on a plain white background, but all that can all be rectified by judicious use of the stylesheet and background images, which we will look at later in this chapter. For now, though, let's concentrate on this logo and how it was placed here. First off, because we have not yet designed the site, and because we would like the site to be as flexible as possible, we created this logo (as we will all other graphics) with a transparent background.

This is always a wise choice unless there is a specific compelling reason to do otherwise, because having a transparent background allows you to make underlying changes to the layout and color scheme of the site without affecting the graphic itself. Just think what a nightmare it would be if all your graphics had a specific color background, and you decided to change the background color of your store—you would have to go and change every single graphic individually to reflect this change.

Now, actually inserting this new GIF file can be a bit of a pest if you don't know where to look. Fortunately, with a bit of searching you will realize that the `header.php` file in the `includes` folder is where this particular log is declared. So, open up this file in your favorite editor and search for the line that reads:

```
<td valign="middle"><?php echo '<a href="' . tep_href_link(FILENAME_DEFAULT) .
'">' . tep_image(DIR_WS_IMAGES . 'oscommerce.gif', 'osCommerce') . '</a>';
?></td>
```

and replace it with the following line (or whatever the name of your new logo is):

```
<td valign="middle"><?php echo '<a href="' . tep_href_link(FILENAME_DEFAULT) .
'">' . tep_image(DIR_WS_IMAGES . 'contechst_books.gif', 'Contechst Books') .
'</a>'; ?></td>
```

As you should be able to tell, this change forces osCommerce to look for the file `contechst_books.gif` instead of `oscommerce.gif` (assuming you have saved it to the `images` directory), and render that to the browser. The second modified value is simply the text that will pop up when the mouse cursor is hovered over this image—in this case we want the name of our store instead of osCommerce.

The same idea applies for inserting any other graphic on the site—you need to find out where it is referenced in the HTML, and then swap the old GIF file for the new one. If you are going to work on your site's logos, then you may as well remember to do the graphics for your packing slips and invoices now too.

Moving and Removing Graphics

Let's begin by talking about how to remove graphics, as this is the easier task to perform. Generally, it involves two steps: find the HTML that inserts the graphic, and then comment it out. Since Contechst Books is not too keen on the use of graphics to echo the functionality offered by text-based links, the three graphics at the top right-hand side of the page, which are used as shortcuts to Your Account, Cart Contents, and Checkout, are going to be removed.

If you haven't closed `header.php` already, then go to the HTML just below the line we modified in the last section and comment it out like so (you may prefer to use PHP comments instead):

```
<!--
    <td align="right" valign="bottom"><?php echo '<a href="' .
tep_href_link(FILENAME_ACCOUNT, '', 'SSL') . '">' . tep_image(DIR_WS_IMAGES .
'header_account.gif', HEADER_TITLE_MY_ACCOUNT) . '</a>  <a href="' .
tep_href_link(FILENAME_SHOPPING_CART) . '">' . tep_image(DIR_WS_IMAGES .
'header_cart.gif', HEADER_TITLE_CART_CONTENTS) . '</a>  <a href="' .
tep_href_link(FILENAME_CHECKOUT_SHIPPING, '', 'SSL') . '">' .
tep_image(DIR_WS_IMAGES . 'header_checkout.gif', HEADER_TITLE_CHECKOUT) .
'</a>'; ?>  </td>
-->
```

This removes the table cell that contains the images and their links so that when you navigate to any page in the site, the heading section will look like this:

Contechst Books

That is really all it takes to remove a graphic from your site—simply find it and comment it out!

Moving graphics can be slightly trickier because you need to fiddle around with the HTML that is responsible for placing them. Let's say, for example, that you had inserted a couple of images onto a page—the following screenshot shows the ebooks and documents section with some new graphics in place:

Now, these graphics are nothing fancy, and I'm sure with a bit of time and effort you will be able to make some that will really uplift the visual aspects of your site. On the development side of things, notice that there is some lightening around the e at the top right at the moment (this may not show up too clearly in your printed copy). This type of issue will be common while you develop your site, and I have purposefully left the image like this because the background color will be a lot lighter in the final product, and this effect will disappear—the point being, always develop with the end goal in mind!

Now, let's assume that we feel that the word Categories is redundant and we wish to replace it with the category image instead. Making this assumption is not unreasonable, since the user will be able to intuit what page they are looking at from its content and layout. All that is left after the text has been removed is to move the graphic across the page to appear on the left of the central column. The same principles apply no matter where you want to place an image; it's simply a case of putting the right HTML in the right place!

Open up index.php in your editor and locate the line that reads:

```
<td class="pageHeading"><?php echo HEADING_TITLE; ?>
```

You should be able to recognize by now that HEADING_TITLE, which in this case holds the word Categories, is defined elsewhere, so there are several options we can use for making that word disappear. You can find out where HEADING_TITLE is defined and change it, or you can remove the entire echo statement, or you can comment out the entire HTML line. So what's the difference? The main difference is really whether you want to keep the same table structure or not. If you don't mind losing the cell, then comment out the whole thing; if you want to keep that cell because you want to place something else there, then perform one of the other operations.

For our purposes it is perfectly OK to remove the line entirely, so the new code looks like this:

```
<!-- <td class="pageHeading"><?php echo HEADING_TITLE; ?> -->
```

Now, of course, comes the big moment, when we move the graphic to its new home on the left-hand side of the screen. The line directly after the one that you have just commented out, reads as follows:

```
<td class="pageHeading" align="right"><?php echo tep_image(DIR_WS_IMAGES .
$category['categories_image'], $category['categories_name'],
HEADING_IMAGE_WIDTH, HEADING_IMAGE_HEIGHT); ?></td>
```

Notice that this is simply a new table cell with the td align attribute set to right. Well, since we want the icon on the left, let's change that attribute and take a look at how this changes the site. The new line should now read:

```
<td class="pageHeading" align="left"><?php echo tep_image(DIR_WS_IMAGES .
$category['categories_image'], $category['categories_name'],
HEADING_IMAGE_WIDTH, HEADING_IMAGE_HEIGHT); ?></td>
```

Saving these changes (plus any comments you wish to insert about the changes) and then viewing the site shows the results are just as we had hoped:

Now that that's done, the only thing left to do is insert graphic files for all the other categories, and your layout work is all done! Well, that's not entirely true... Click on another category—one that doesn't have subcategories. You will see that the icon has been realigned on the right—this means for those categories the alignment is set somewhere else. The best thing to do is search the index.php file for the string align="right", and sure enough, you will find the culprit, which can then be modified to show the graphic on the left-hand side of the screen.

Of course, there are countless possibilities for placing graphics wherever you want. All that's required is a bit of patience and some time to play around with the HTML. There is, however, one other type of image that is going to play a role in the Contechst Books site and we look at that next.

Background Images

One of the nicest things about designing sites (in my humble opinion) is that you can use whatever image-making software you choose for designing unbelievable pictures, which can then be very easily incorporated into your site. This ability to design on specialist software and then add to your HTML is a critical feature, without which it would soon become quite distressing to create pleasing background images.

Backgrounds themselves can be quite tricky to get right if you are using them for sections of pages that resize. If you know a page section will always be the same size, then you can design your background to order and there need not be any further fuss. If your page is going to resize, then you need to keep this in mind when creating the background image so that you don't end up with terribly distorted or ill-fitting pictures.

Now, Contechst Books would like to create a background image for the site's heading. Obviously, if your background image relies on knowing the width of the page section you are catering to (say, the left-hand column), the first thing to do is find out how wide that column is. Incidentally, by default it is set to 125 pixels, which is slightly too narrow for Contechst's liking. So, locating the BOX_WIDTH setting in the application_top.php file and setting it to 150 will give us a slightly wider box to work with and also tells us how wide to make our background image at the same time.

There are a few things to keep in mind when creating a background image apart from the width of the page section. Length is also a concern because if you have a really long page, you will end up repeating the image, which can look really untidy if it is not planned for. One solution is to create a large background that will cover all the possible area your site could expand to, but then you need to think carefully about how large this image is going to be—remember, anything over a handful of kilobytes is too much and will contribute to slowing down your site.

You can, of course, create small background images that can be repeated over and over to fill up the screen, but by and large it is best to use background for areas you are certain will not change drastically. In our case, the heading section looks pretty boring as it stands, so we are going to create a background that will fill up the empty (for now) space in the heading section:

As you can see, this has quite a nice effect on the bar, and the background image can be made as small as you like because it simply repeats every time it runs out of width—since it doesn't change on the horizontal, it looks like one seamless striping of the main navigation bar. Of course, it is quite possible that the main navigation bar will undergo changes, but changing the background image to reflect this is very easy to do.

Notice also why it was important to make the background of the company's title logo transparent. Without doing that, the area under the title would appear as whatever background color was set, and not as the background image. Let's quickly look at how to work with button images before moving on to the section on customizing the stylesheet, where we will actually insert the background image we created in this section.

Button Images

Of course, there are plenty of ways to create buttons, and you might find you want to use Flash or some other software to create exciting, dynamic buttons for your site. Remember too that some special effects can also be achieved through the use of the stylesheet, so you are not totally doomed to using static-looking buttons if you don't want to go through the trouble of learning how to use other software products.

The buttons provided by osCommerce are fairly innocuous, and will certainly do the trick if you are happy to go ahead and use them. However, you should at least take a look at all the available options, which can be found online and in the community contributions. Working on the buttons yourself will also be a great exercise and will certainly boost your graphics-related experience. The flip side is that there are plenty of nice buttons out there that are free for you to use, so why not just use them instead of reinventing the wheel?

For those of you who *do* wish to work on your buttons by hand, you will find the relevant images in the `includes\languages\english\images\buttons` folder instead of with the rest of the images. This is because the buttons themselves depend on the language the site is working in, of course, and you will have to make the same modifications to all the buttons in all the languages you wish to present your site in. Simply create a button image for each type of button that is already in place, back up the current button files, and replace them with the new ones.

For the Contechst Books site, some buttons that are available under the GPL, or GNU General Public License, were used to smarten up the feel of the site. These particular ones were available, at the time of writing, at `http://kalsey.com/2003/10/oscommerce_button_set/`, and were made available by Adam Kalsey. A screenshot of the site, with the new buttons, will follow in the next section.

Incidentally, you might wish to quickly page over to Chapter 7 where we discuss how to create button templates, which you can then use anywhere in your site whenever you have the need for a new button.

Customizations Using the Stylesheet

Pages in osCommerce obtain their style-related information from the associated stylesheet entitled `stylesheet.css`, found in the `catalog` folder. Using stylesheets gives you excellent, fine-grained control over the appearance of your web pages, and even allows you to produce some great effects. The appearance of pretty much every aspect of the site can be controlled from here, and all that is needed is a little knowledge of fonts, colors, and stylesheet syntax.

Before we go any further, it will make life easier if you have a readymade list of the type of things you should look at setting using the stylesheet. The following is a list of the most common areas (defined by HTML elements) where stylesheets can be used to determine the look and feel of a site:

- Background
- Text
- Font
- Border
- Margin
- Padding
- List

As well as being able to change all these aspects of HTML, you can also apply different effects depending on 'whether or not' conditions like a mouse cursor hovering over the specified area—as will be demonstrated a little later on. You can also specify attributes for certain HTML tags, which can then be used to apply stylesheet styles to those specific tags instead of creating application-wide changes. For example, if you had one paragraph style with a `class` attribute set, like so:

```
<p class="center"></p>
```

then you could specify this type of paragraph in your stylesheet explicitly by saying something like:

```
p.center { color: green; }
```

Analyzing this line highlights the structure of the standard stylesheet code block, which appears in the form:

- **Selector**: In this case `p.center`
- **Property**: In this case `color`
- **Delimiter**: Always `:`
- **Value**: In this case `green`

All the property/value pairs are contained within curly braces, and are ended with a semi-colon. Now, without getting too carried away in the niceties of stylesheets, let's finish off the bulk of the modifications to the visual part of the site using the stylesheet. In your favorite editor, open up `stylesheet.css`, and let's begin…

Inserting Background Images

In order to insert the background image that was shown in the last section, the following modification was made to the stylesheet:

```
/* Background image added */
TR.header {
  background: #ffffff;
  background-image: url('images/heading_background.gif');
}
```

Make a similar change to your stylesheet using your background image—or any image for that matter, since you just want to ensure that something is inserted into the background. Take a look at your site, and you should notice that the header of each page now has a background image. Simple? Not always… It can be quite tricky to know which modification to make and in what place. For this, you have to find out how all the HTML elements have been created. For example, open up `header.php` and look for the line:

```
<tr class="header">
```

Can you see why the above modification affected only the header section of the page? It's because the class declaration for this particular tr HTML tag has been given the class header, which is then defined in the stylesheet using the TR.header selector. Adding background images anywhere in your code is therefore simply a case of locating the right HTML tag and shoving it in. Remember, though, that not all tags have the same properties—a paragraph tag <p> doesn't have a background-image property, for example.

As an exercise, try inserting an image into one infobox heading without having it placed in all of them.

Changing Colors and Fonts

There are a lot of interesting things to be done on the color front. You can change the color of any area of the screen with only minimal effort. Since the demo site needs to fit in with its parent site, we are going to go with the gray, black, and red color scheme with only minor hints of other colors here and there. There is not really much point in rattling off a long list of all the modifications made to get the color scheme to this point:

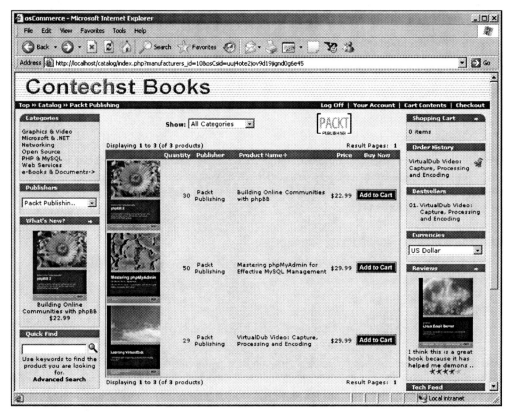

Notice some of the more interesting modifications to the stylesheet (as well as the addition of the new buttons).

The body background color:

```
BODY {
  background: #EAEAEA;
  color: #000000;
  margin: 0px;
}
```

The header section:

```
TR.header {
  background-image: url('images/heading_background.gif');
}
```

The navigation bar:

```
TD.headerNavigation {
  font-family: Verdana, Arial, sans-serif;
  font-size: 10px;
  background: #003366;
  color: #ffffff;
  font-weight : bold;
  border: 0px;
  border-bottom-width: 1px;
  border-style: solid;
  border-color: #B7B7B7;
}
```

The infobox content sections:

```
.infoBoxContents {
  background: #E0E0E0;
  font-family: Verdana, Arial, sans-serif;
  font-size: 10px;
}
```

There are quite a few other changes that were made, but the above list should show you enough to get the idea. For more information on using stylesheets, try Google, or go to http://www.w3schools.com/css/.

Now, there is one thing concerning changes made to the background colors that needs mentioning quickly. In order to get that rounded effect on some of the infobox heading bars, graphic images were used. Namely, corner_left.gif, corner_right.gif, corner_right_left.gif, and arrow_right.gif, which are housed in the images\infobox folder. So, if you wish to change the color of the background for the TD.infoBoxHeading HTML elements, you will need to change these GIF files accordingly lest you end up with odd looking corners.

Fonts get much the same treatment as the colors used in the site in general. One of the really interesting effects for text that is used in HTML links is the hover effect. Take a look in the stylesheet at the code block which reads:

```
A:hover {
  color: #AABBDD;
  text-decoration: underline;
}
```

Given the color scheme of the demo site, we really want to change this color so that when the mouse cursor is hovered over a link, the color changes to something more apparent. Modify the code to look like this, and then point your mouse over the navigation links on a refreshed page:

```
A:hover {
  color: #F79418;
  text-decoration: underline;
}
```

Since that color does not really suit the color of the link in the navigation bar (don't ask me why, it just doesn't), you can try the following changes to the hover property of the navigation text:

```
A.headerNavigation:hover {
  color: #F79418;
}
```

This gives the link text a Packt-ish kind of feel (in other words, orange), which we all like!

Of course, you can always change the actual font properties of the font, instead of simply playing around with the colors. You can bold and underline to your heart's content. Such changes should really be done to taste, and if you get stuck, search for the answers online. For now, the demo site is quite happy with the fonts as they are.

Before we leave stylesheets, remember that it is very important to test your entire site thoroughly; it is almost impossible to predict what effect every single little change will have on your site. You might find that error messages, for example, pop up in a totally different color and font than the rest of your site because you never modified them earlier—this is an easy mistake to make, because not all text or HTML elements are visible all the time.

Even worse, a few colors are not defined in the stylesheet but are instead done using <span> tags directly in the language files. This happens, for example, on the login-page default text. You simply have to look over your site very carefully and ensure that you have modified everything accordingly.

Miscellaneous Customizations

There are an indefinite number of adjustments or additions that you can make to the site—your imagination is the real limit in this respect. However, there are a few that deserve special mention because they are the most common. Remember that while we have only a bit of space to talk about some of the more important customizations, someone else has probably had to solve whatever customization problem you might have already. Make sure you use the online community to help you out if you get stuck.

Resizing Pages

The demo site needs to limit the size of the current pages to a determined width in order to provide space for some advertising, which is to appear down the right-hand side of the page. You might find that you wish to limit the width of your pages to keep everything compact and neat—especially if you have decided on a minimalist page design, which would look sparse on a large screen. Many companies do limit their page sizes for a variety of reasons, so it is important to have some control over your site's page sizes.

In order to accomplish this task, we need to say goodbye to the stylesheet and begin working directly on the page HTML. For the sake of demonstration, we will work on the index page and allow the central column to resize up to a limit of 600 pixels. After that the page will stop expanding, and users who are viewing the page on full screen will instead be able to view adverts running down the right-hand side.

Keep in mind that osCommerce does not have a unified page sizing facility. In other words, whatever page modifications you make to one of you pages, you will need to record and implement on all the other pages that you wish to have the same behavior. This is a bit of a drag, but it really isn't difficult to do with a bit of copying and pasting.

To begin with, open up `index.php` in your editor and search for the line that reads:

```
<table border="0" width="100%" cellspacing="3" cellpadding="3">
```

somewhere around line 49. This tag controls the overall width of the page, which you can see by examining the width tag, which is set to fill out the entire screen by always being 100%. You have another option in that you can set an absolute value in terms of the number of pixels to be used. For example, change the line to the following and then examine your page in a variety of different sizes:

```
<table border="0" width="800" cellspacing="3" cellpadding="3">
```

You will probably notice a problem with this page immediately. If you increase the page size above the 800 pixel mark, then the header and footer sections keep expanding leaving your page looking something like this:

This is pretty untidy, and we obviously would like to make the page stop expanding at the same point above and below. This means we are going to have to edit the `header.php` and `footer.php` files to reflect this change in width. So, open up both pages and in `header.php` look for the lines that read:

```
<table border="0" width="100%" cellspacing="0" cellpadding="1">
```

and:

```
<table border="0" width="100%" cellspacing="0" cellpadding="2">
```

somewhere near lines 55 and 63 respectively, and change them to the new width like so:

```
<table border="0" width="800" cellspacing="0" cellpadding="1">
...
<table border="0" width="800" cellspacing="0" cellpadding="2">
```

Then, in the footer you will need to change three table widths instead of two. Notice that unless the tables are set to the same width, the copyright message and the banner will shift further and further to the right as the page width increases. Accordingly, you should change the width attribute for all the tables (not just the first one) in the `footer.php` file to 800 pixels. This is because the alignment of the text and banner content is set to be `center`, and unless these table are all set to have the same length, the footer can end up looking skewed—like this:

Once those changes are all made, go along to the Conditions of Use page (conditions.php) and take a look—you should see something like this:

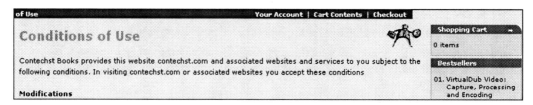

Oh dear! That's not very good... Remember that you have to modify the HTML for every different page to reflect the changes made to the site. Once you have worked out how to make the changes to one page, simply copying them over to all the others is an easy task.

What we have demonstrated here is a pretty simple modification to your standard site pages. Of course, you may wish to effect far more grand or sweeping changes to your site, and whatever changes to the HTML you need to make, the process is exactly the same as the one we have outlined—with one additional warning!

> Be aware that each PHP page may contain several versions of the same page, depending on the state of the session. If this is the case, you need to modify all the versions of each page within the same PHP file, so make sure you check everything thoroughly.

A case in point is in fact the index page, which displays a default page, as well as other information based on user requests. Some changes to the HTML will be applied to one version only, and not the page as a whole, so you need to check the presentation on both the default and result versions of that page.

Adding Pages

Of course, it is pretty likely that at some stage, as your online site grows, you will find that you want to present more pages than the ones provided by default. In such a case, you need to add a new page with all the correct layout information and HTML elements in place. The best way to do this is to copy a page that most closely resembles what you want the new page to look like, and then save it in the catalog folder under its new name.

For this example, we will take the `shipping.php` file and turn it into the `feed.php` file, which will be linked to from either a click on the feed box or from the Information box on the bottom left of the page. Open up `shipping.php` and save a copy as `feed.php` in the `catalog` folder. That's it! You now have a new page, which you can confirm is working by modifying its content as follows:

```
<td><table border="0" width="100%" cellspacing="0" cellpadding="0">
    <tr>
        <td class="pageHeading"><?php echo "What's New In Technology"; ?></td>
        <td class="pageHeading" align="right"><?php echo tep_image
            (DIR_WS_IMAGES . 'table_background_specials.gif',
            HEADING_TITLE, HEADING_IMAGE_WIDTH, HEADING_IMAGE_HEIGHT); ?></td>
```

and navigating to it in your browser:

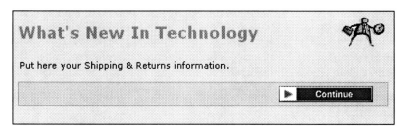

At the moment, this isn't too helpful, and we have done something *wrong* in terms of developing with osCommerce conventions in mind. Can you tell what it is? Instead of allowing the new `feed.php` page to call the `HEADING_TITLE` constant, which all the other pages do, we simply inserted our own What's New In Technology text to prove we had the right page. It's no biggie, but we should make the proper changes anyway. So, return the `feed.php` file to its original state, and open up the `shipping.php` file in the `includes/languages/english/` folder, save a copy as `feed.php`, and make the following changes:

```
define('NAVBAR_TITLE', 'Technology Feed');
define('HEADING_TITLE', 'What\'s new in Technology?');
define('TEXT_INFORMATION', 'This is the future site of the RSS tech feed.');
```

Once this is done, close this file and open up the `feed.php` file in the `catalog` directory. We need to tell `feed.php` where to look to pick up the definitions we have just created, and this involves making changes to the following line:

```
require(DIR_WS_LANGUAGES . $language . '/' . FILENAME_SHIPPING);
$breadcrumb->add(NAVBAR_TITLE, tep_href_link(FILENAME_SHIPPING));
```

Of course, these constants are the ones used for the `shipping.php` file, and are defined in the `includes/filenames.php` file. We need to make our own definitions for this file within the `filenames.php` file, so we open that up as well and add the following line to the bottom of the page:

```
define('FILENAME_FEED', 'feed.php');
```

Save that change and then modify the `feed.php` file to pick up the `includes/languages/english/feed.php` file via the `FILENAME_FEED` constant, like so:

```
require(DIR_WS_LANGUAGES . $language . '/' . FILENAME_FEED);
$breadcrumb->add(NAVBAR_TITLE, tep_href_link(FILENAME_FEED));
```

Now when you navigate to the feed page, it should have no traces of its former self left:

Notice that the bread crumb trail now reflects the fact that this is the technology-feed page, and the heading is being picked up via the constant instead of the original message typed directly into the file. With this done, the page is ready to be used as you wish, but we will only begin working on it later. The only thing left to do (if you wish) is add this page to the information bar. This can be done quite easily by a few simple modifications.

First, open up english.php in the Define Languages section of the admin tool, and make the following addition:

```
// information box text in includes/boxes/information.php
define('BOX_HEADING_INFORMATION', 'Information');
define('BOX_INFORMATION_PRIVACY', 'Privacy Notice');
define('BOX_INFORMATION_CONDITIONS', 'Conditions of Use');
define('BOX_INFORMATION_SHIPPING', 'Shipping & Returns');
define('BOX_INFORMATION_CONTACT', 'Contact Us');
define('BOX_INFORMATION_FEED', 'Technology Feed');
```

Save that and then in the includes/boxes/information.php file, make the following changes:

```
    $info_box_contents[] = array('text' =>
'<a href="' . tep_href_link(FILENAME_SHIPPING) . '">' .
BOX_INFORMATION_SHIPPING . '</a><br>' .
'<a href="' . tep_href_link(FILENAME_PRIVACY) . '">' . BOX_INFORMATION_PRIVACY
. '</a><br>' .
'<a href="' . tep_href_link(FILENAME_CONDITIONS) . '">' .
BOX_INFORMATION_CONDITIONS . '</a><br>' .
'<a href="' . tep_href_link(FILENAME_CONTACT_US) . '">' .
BOX_INFORMATION_CONTACT . '</a><br>' .
'<a href="' . tep_href_link(FILENAME_FEED, '', 'NONSSL') . '">' .
BOX_INFORMATION_FEED . '</a>'
```

Now when you view the Information box in your browser, you get the following:

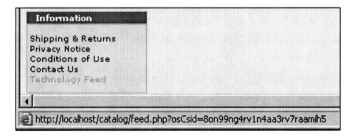

Notice that the status bar at the bottom of the screen shows that the highlighted link Technology Feed will take the customer to the feed.php file as expected. What you actually use the page for now is entirely up to you, but the process is the same for any page added.

Emails

Emails are an important interface between the customer and your business, and of course you will need to make some changes here and there to suit your site. Several different types of emails can be sent out from your store. These are the purchase confirmation, tell a friend, and welcome emails as well as the newsletters. The first three are very easy to change by simply editing them in the Language Definitions section of the admin tool—the files to modify are checkout_process.php, tell_a_friend.php, and create_account.php respectively.

The newsletter is slightly different in that you work with it through the Newsletter Manager in the admin tool. Using the tool is pretty easy; simply click on New Newsletter and add the information you want. You can choose one of two types of newsletter modules by default from the drop-down list in the New Newsletter editor. Choosing newsletter makes life simple because the store already knows which customers have chosen to receive the newsletter. Once you have written it out, you can preview, edit, delete, or send it provided it is locked. If it is unlocked, you can only preview or lock it; you can't change it in any way.

If you choose product_notification, then you need to inform osCommerce which product(s) this notification is linked to so that it can send it off to the right people. As a result, when you click on send, you are brought to the following page:

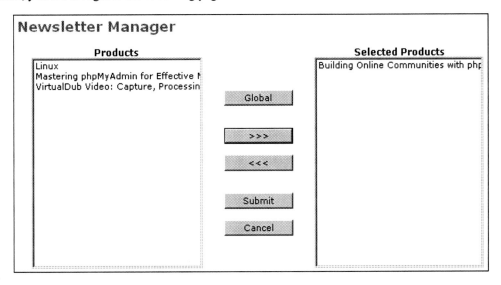

From here, you can select which products this notification is linked to—there is also a Global option to send it to all if need be. Once you have made your choices and clicked on submit, you will get the following confirmation screen, which you can use to check everything one last time before sending it out:

Of course, you may not always be happy sending out plain text emails. What happens if you would like to start sending out images of your new products in a monthly newsletter? The answer is to simply go along to the contributions section and add a **WYSIWYG (What You See Is What You Get)** editor for your newsletters. One package that you might want to look at, to begin with, is the MS2 HTML WYSIWYG Editor, Product Desc, Email + contribution, which can be found in the Features section or with a search on the term newsletter.

Summary

This chapter represents a great percentage of the overall work required to get your site looking as you want it. Once you are finished with this section, you will hopefully be satisfied that you are well on your way to a working site. A site, which will contribute to increased revenue through customers' confidence in the site's professionalism and design, as well as providing a pleasing environment in which they can make purchases.

The knowledge gained from working with images and HTML will help not only with your osCommerce site, but with any other web-based application that you end up working with. Having gained an appreciation for the various different types of customization, as well as having to work closely with GIF images, will free you up to create more ambitious graphical user interfaces in the future.

Now that you have the necessary information to make your site look professional, we need to actually make it professional. When I talk about professional, I mean getting paid, so let's take a look at how to deal with tax, payment, and shipping issues.

6

Taxes, Payments, and Shipping

Having reached this section of the development phase of your online store, you are permitted now to rub your hands together in a greedy fashion. Fundamentally, we all need to ensure a stable, if not always hugely profitable, source of income from our endeavors if we are to be able to realize our goals. Providing an excellent online avenue for sales, which makes it easy for customers to purchase goods from the comfort of their own homes, and which gives you, the merchant, the mouth-watering opportunity to sell to customers anywhere and any time is what e-commerce is all about.

To this end, osCommerce comes with a host of installable modules, which handle the complexities inherent in securing a variety of different payment types. As you would expect from software such as osCommerce, much thought and knowledge has gone into making the payment side of things as easy and efficient as possible. Try to imagine how much work would be involved in obtaining sensitive customers information, validating it all, protecting it from other parties, and integrating it with the rest of your application if it wasn't for our good friends at osCommerce.

> Despite the fair amount of work required to get a new osCommerce installation up and running, the fact that building a fully fledged e-commerce site is now within the grasp of the average businessman is an excellent contribution to the world of commerce as a whole, and especially to those with limited resources.

Watch out though—hidden dangers lurk at every corner for the unsuspecting online merchant, and unless you know precisely what you are doing, you should really stick to the more secure forms of payment rather than attempting to run a full-blown merchant account and unwittingly allowing malicious intruders access to sensitive financial information. On the other hand, the last thing you want to do is come all this way only to have to force customers to pay by check or bank deposit and so on. So where is the balance?

This chapter will attempt to give you the right balance in terms of the approach it takes in covering this material. For completeness, we will discuss all of the most common methods of receiving revenue from sales, but emphasis will be placed on the use of PayPal, since this is easy, well known, and well respected, and also supports a range of payment methods. All other options are recommended behind PayPal, with some, like handling your own merchant account, not being recommended at all for reasons of security and safety.

Of course, getting paid is not the whole story. You still have to make sure that you can get the product to the customer as well as make it as painless as possible on their wallets. This naturally requires a bit of thought about who will be buying what and from where, but once you have a good idea, it is not too hard to get all your ducks in a row.

Accordingly, this chapter will discuss:

- Locations and taxes
- PayPal payments
- Credit-card payments
- Alternative forms of payment—checks/money orders and cash on delivery
- Shipping

What we are aiming for really when we set up the various methods of payment is to have the transactions executed securely, reliably, and with some form of recovery in case things go awry somewhere along the line. Managing your payments effectively and reliably, as well as incorporating the correct shipping method and charges, is obviously one of the largest contributing factors to generating even more successful business transactions as well as happy customers along the way. Pay very careful attention to this section because you can really hurt your business by not being on the ball when it comes to taking people's hard-earned money.

Locations and Taxes

It is appropriate at this point to discuss the Locations/Taxes section in the admin tool because the settings here impact directly on your payment and shipping policies. By this stage, you have had plenty of practice using the admin tool, so I won't hold you up too much with a long discussion. Instead, we will look at the available settings and relate them to what you need for your business.

The default page, Countries, simply gives a list of all the ISO country codes. It's a useful reference if you decide to use a zone-based shipping policy, because you will need to enter various country codes into your zone-based shipping table.

The next page, Zones, gives a list of the more common zones or regions in Europe and North America, which is useful for osCommerce users. For example, there is a zone code for each of the states in the US, including some overseas territories. These can be used while determining which zones you will ship to, or what tax policy to implement—you will see an example of this later on when we deal with zone rates.

The next option is worth looking at in a little more depth because it can be slightly confusing how to work with Tax Zones.

Tax Zones

By default we are given a zone called Florida, which has the description Florida local sales tax zone. But what if you don't live in Florida and don't need to worry about Florida's tax laws? By way of example, let's assume we are in California and wish to enter that region into the system for tax purposes.

On the **Tax Zones** homepage, click on insert, and in the textboxes provided, give a name and description for your new tax zone. The following screenshot shows the result of the demo site's modification:

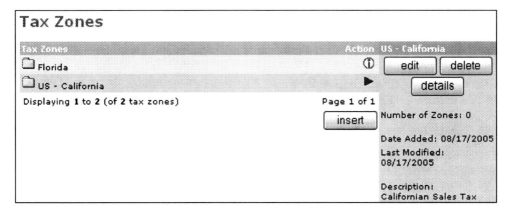

We aren't done yet, because this has not actually associated any zone with the name and description we have just entered. In order to do this, we must click on details and then select the subzone, or subzones, that fall under this category. Click on insert when the next page comes up, and then enter the country and zone you wish to link to this tax zone's name. I don't suppose you need to be told to make the name as accurate as possible so that you know which tax zone is associated with which zones. In our case we have, quite intuitively, added California as shown here:

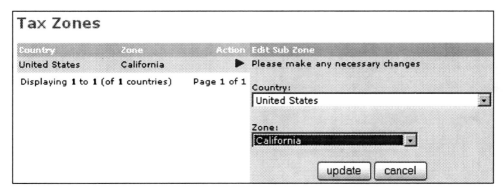

Of course, you can associate more than one subzone with each tax zone you name, and how you set things up should be the result of a bit of trial and error along with some research. For our purposes this is fine, and if you want to have a quick peek at how this zone can now be used, then go along to the **Table Rate** shipping module in the **Modules** section of the admin tool and install (if it's not already installed) and edit the module. You will notice you have a shipping option as follows:

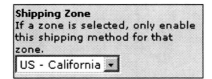

This is not the only place where a zone set by you comes into play. For example, in the payment modules you will find the following option:

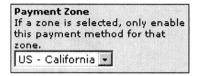

Of course, setting tax zones is all good and well, but up till now we haven't looked at how to actually classify various products in terms of tax. The next section deals with precisely that.

Tax Classes and Rates

Setting your tax class works in much the same way as setting the tax zone. You need to come up with a tax class name along with a good description for it. Once you have saved that, simply click on Tax Rates to bring up the page that allows you to set your tax percentage for that particular category. For example, the demo site added the DaylightRobbery tax in Tax Class, and then after clicking new tax rate on the Tax Rate the page was edited to get the following results:

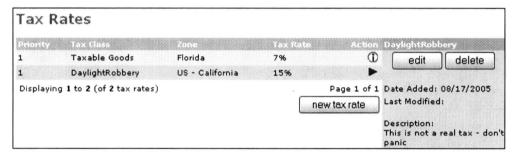

Now, if you have products that fall under the DaylightRobbery tax scheme, then you can tell osCommerce to add this tax to the products' gross price when you edit the products' attributes in the Catalog section of the admin tool, like so:

Observe now that the highlighted value gives the gross product price based on a calculation of 15% of $22.99, which is what we would expect from our DaylightRobbery tax. In this way you can exert fine-grained control over the taxing of all your products, which is especially useful if you are working with exotic products.

Depending on your geographical location, nationality, and the types of products you are dealing with, you will need to think carefully about how to deal with your tax responsibilities. Remember that your internal revenue service can be of assistance as well as the osCommerce community in this regard. With that done, let's move on to far more happier thoughts like…

Getting Paid with PayPal

Businesses of any size can benefit from the reliable and trusted PayPal brand. Using PayPal for osCommerce transactions, you use one of the easier modules to work with. In fact, you can have a more or less working PayPal facility up and running in no time at all. The hard work comes from ironing out the wrinkles along the way and ensuring the smoothest operation of your payments in the future.

If you are happy with the most basic setup, then all you need to do is create your own PayPal account, and enable the PayPal module in osCommerce using the admin tool. Then, when customers attempt to purchase goods, they will have the option to pay with PayPal and be redirected to the PayPal site, where they can make the transaction.

There are a couple of problems to doing things this way! The main thing is that customers making payment might simply close their browser, without continuing back to the store. In this case, the order is simply not recorded in the database. This is clearly quite a problem because straightaway you will be unsure as to who has paid for what without manually checking your records. Secondly, customers must have a PayPal account in order to complete the transaction—this is not necessarily the case if you decide to implement PayPal functionality on your own because PayPal has now introduced Account Optional facilities.

As of milestone 2, version 2.2, there is a contribution that uses the PayPal IPN system to make transactions secure and reliable. This is what we are going to use for the example site, so head on over to the contribution's homepage and download it from `http://www.osCommerce.com/ community/contributions,2679`.

> This is a community contribution, and is subject to upgrades and changes. As a result of this, you may not use exactly the same version as shown here. At the time of writing, the recommended version is the one uploaded on the 6th of August by judebert.

Some of you may be asking, "What is an IPN?"

Well, very briefly, let's quickly go over the payment transaction process for PayPal to get a good idea of what is going on under the hood. From the PayPal website, the definition of an IPN is:

Instant Payment Notification (IPN) is PayPal's interface for handling real-time purchase confirmation and server-to-server communications. IPN delivers immediate notification and confirmation of PayPal payments you receive and provides status and additional data on pending, cancelled, or failed transactions.

Basically, an IPN is sent to your server as soon as a payment is made, allowing you to incorporate information sent with this notification into your programming. On receiving the notification, your server will send the information, including the encrypted code, back to a secure PayPal URL. PayPal will then authenticate the transaction and send your server a *Verified* or *Invalid* response, which you can use to fulfill an order after you have performed a few checks.

Now, you don't even have to have any form of security enabled to do this because there is no sensitive client information being passed back and forth between your server and PayPal. But while this is an option, you shouldn't really treat it as such—consequently, from your point of view, you either need to have encryption enabled to work with PayPal or you must have a secure server that can be targeted by PayPal.

As well as this, in order to get the IPN system functional you need to be able to supply PayPal with a valid URL, which it will use to send its messages to. For now, though, let's begin with setting up a PayPal account…

Setting Up PayPal on osCommerce

It's very easy to set up your PayPal account. Simply head along to http://www.paypal.com, click on Sign up, and select the type of account you wish to create—more than likely a business or premier account. You will then have to furnish PayPal with a bunch of details about yourself and your business, and confirm all this before you will be given an account. Once that is done, you will be presented with a screen that looks much like this:

At some stage you will need to have your account verified, which will allow you to lift the limit on the amount of funds that can be withdrawn from your new account. Everything in this interface is reasonably self explanatory, and you are advised to spend some time learning your way around it before continuing. Assuming you have got your account to the status and state you need it in so as to run your business, you can turn to the admin tool and install the PayPal module in the Modules/Payments section, like so:

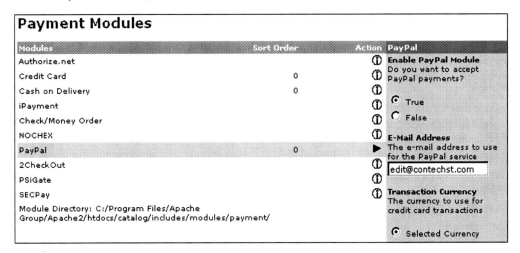

With that done, you can check to see whether everything is working by purchasing an item from the site and ensuring you are taken to the correct PayPal page to make the payment. Unless you have a couple of accounts, you will either be unable to pay yourself, or you will end up having to pay from your own account into your business account, so it isn't recommended you take it any further than this at this stage.

Unfortunately, this is not the end of the story because in order to make sure that the payments work smoothly without us having to verify orders manually, we are going to have to use the PayPal IPN contribution.

Connecting osCommerce and PayPal

The first step here is to install the IPN contribution, which requires you to copy files into the catalog directory. Please read the instructions supplied with the contribution to ensure that you copy everything across properly. Once this is done, you can simply go to the Payment page in the Modules section of the administration tool and click install. (Remember to remove the other PayPal module at the same time.) This will bring up a list of options, which you will need to edit.

For simplicity's sake we will show you how to get a live site up and running (so you know it can be done). In reality you will need to do some testing before using the live PayPal server. In order to perform some testing you need to register as a developer with PayPal, at http://developer.paypal.com, and make use of their sandbox site. There is plenty of advice and documentation to help you on your way, so we won't cover it further here.

You can use the PayPal IPN contribution to choose whether to use the live site or the developer's sandbox to process transactions by simply changing the Gateway Server option to Testing instead of Live. Remember that when you do your testing work you will need to create several accounts—one to act as the receiver of payments, and a few buyers.

Let's get back to the live site. By now you should have the IPN contribution installed and the default module disabled. You should edit the module appropriately according to your circumstances. For example, you might have something like the following setup:

Property	Setting
Enable PayPal IPN Module Do you want to accept PayPal IPN payments?	This is obviously set to True.
E-Mail Address The e-mail address to use for the PayPal IPN service	The email address of your PayPal account at which you wish to receive your store's payments.
Transaction Currency The currency to use for transactions	This was left as Select Currency, but you will need to decide this based on your payment criteria.
Payment Zone If a zone is selected, only enable this payment method for that zone.	Since we are happy to receive payments via PayPal from anywhere in the world, this was left as none.
Set Preparing Order Status Set the status of prepared orders made with this payment module to this value	This was set to Preparing [PayPal IPN] instead of Processing in order to distinguish it from the default module.
Set PayPal Completed Order Status Set the status of orders made with this payment module to this value	This was set to Processing, but can be changed to any of the values in the drop-down list depending on how you want to structure your payments. For example, you might want to take certain actions based on the status of an order, in which case set this (along with other the status of other payments) to the status you desire.
Set PayPal Denied/Refunded Order Status Set a specific status to denote that something has gone wrong	A new status, Denied, was used here. You can add it to the drop-down list by going to Localization	Orders Status in the admin tool and adding a Denied status there. This option is then available for you to use in all your payment modules.
Gateway Server Use the testing (sandbox) or live gateway server for transactions?	You will obviously use the sandbox for some time until you are happy everything is working as it should. For the purposes of this demonstration, though, it has been set to Live.
Transaction Type Send individual items to PayPal or aggregate all as one total item?	This was set to Aggregate since we want entire orders processed in one go.

Property	Setting
Page Style The page style to use for the transaction procedure (defined at your PayPal profile page)	You can set the look and feel of your personal PayPal payment page from the your account's page by selecting the Custom Payment Pages option in the Seller Preferences category of the Profile section—in this case it has been set to contechst, which you will see shortly.
Debug E-Mail Address All parameters of an Invalid IPN notification will be sent to this email address if one is entered.	Decide on an email address on which you can receive notifications of any IPN irregularities.
Sort order of display Sort order of display. Lowest is displayed first.	This is a standard option and simply governs the order in which the modules are presented on the payment information page.

Incidentally, due to the nature of dealing with downloadable products, many of the order status settings shown in the preceding table will be changed in the *Working with Downloadable Products* section in Chapter 7.

> It is strongly recommended that you take a look at Chapter 7 before finalizing your order statuses even if you aren't going to work with downloadable products. This is because the way in which order statuses can be manipulated is covered in some detail there and will provide you with a more sophisticated way of controlling your purchases.

Also, we haven't covered the encryption section of this module's settings because we will deal with that on its own in Chapter 7. Saving the above settings with their appropriate values and ignoring the rest, we can move to the next task. Common wisdom has it that you need to tell PayPal where it is that it should be sending its notifications... or do you? Actually, this contribution is really meant to take pretty much all responsibility off your hands, and you don't even have to tell PayPal where it needs to send its IPN.

This may seem slightly confusing to some of you who have already worked with PayPal previously because it is recommended that you supply a target address under the Profile section of your PayPal account page. I will show the standard process here because it highlights a couple of points, but please bear in mind that you *don't need to do this* if you are using the PayPal IPN module.

Under other circumstances, you would set things up on the PayPal side by clicking on the Profile link on your PayPal account page and then navigating to the Instant Payment Notification Preferences under the Selling Preferences heading. Once you are there, edit the settings like so (obviously substituting the correct values for your server):

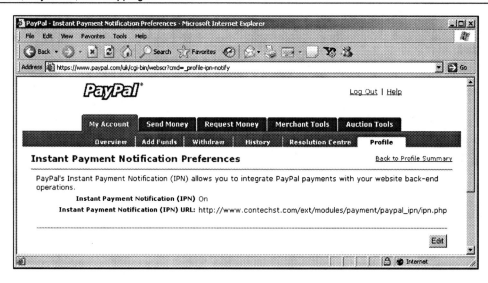

Two things you will notice here:

The first is why we needed a live site to work with PayPal—obviously a development machine will have no way of receiving IPNs from PayPal, so only a working URL (shown here as http://www.contechst.com) will do. Second, we have told PayPal to send payments to the ipn.php file in the ext/modules/payment/paypal_ipn/ folder. This location might change depending on the version of the IPN contribution you are using.

Now, in contrast to this, the target URL for PayPal is actually passed to PayPal by the IPN payment module as part of the request, which is why we don't need to perform any actions other than installing the module. A customer can then select this payment method off the site, be redirected to PayPal, and can make the payment. You can verify this by observing the various stages of the order in the Orders section of the admin tool.

Working with PayPal

That's everything you need to do to get osCommerce talking to PayPal and making everything work nice and smoothly—easy! Let's run through the whole process step by step so that everything is clear at this point. First, a customer gets to the following stage on the site:

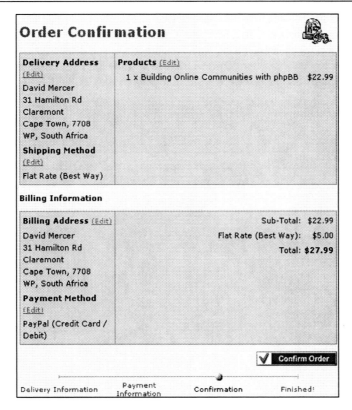

Notice that the customer has selected the PayPal (Credit Card/ Debit) payment option, and that the total price of the purchase is $27.99. Once the Confirm Order button is clicked, the customer is redirected to the PayPal site to complete the payment. If, however, we take a look at the admin tool, we see that it has already picked up on the fact that we are, in all likelihood, about to receive a payment via PayPal, and the screen looks like this:

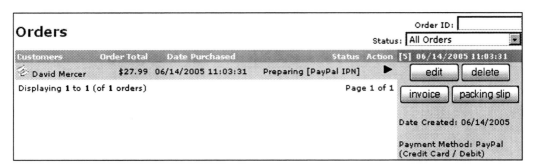

Now, the Status message is set during the editing of the IPN payment module as you have already seen earlier in the table presented. So, at this stage, osCommerce knows what is coming in terms of the type of payment that is being made, and it's waiting on the customer to go through and make the payment. Assuming the customer does just this, he or she will be presented with the following customized page (recall that this setting was also made when editing the IPN payment module):

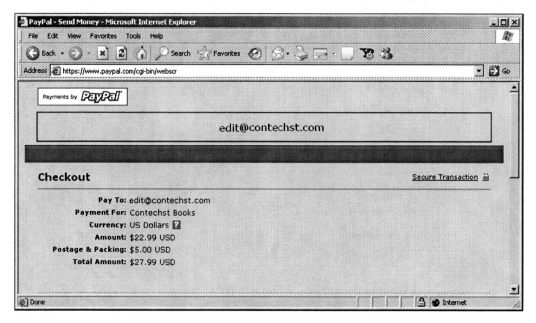

Of course, this is just a demo to show that you can control the look and feel of the PayPal page so that it provides a more seamless transition between your site and PayPal for customers. Once the payment has been made, we can look at the order in more detail. You will notice that there is now a new section, which shows the status of the IPN, towards the bottom of the screen:

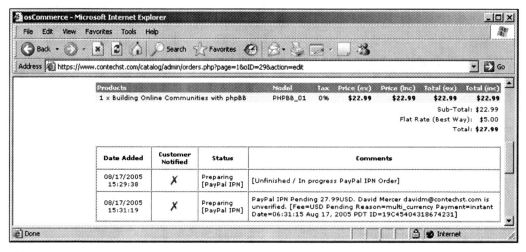

The first two status rows actually get added between the purchasing of the product on the site and the acceptance of payment by the merchant once the customer has paid. Of course, to confirm all this, you should receive an email from PayPal informing you that you have received a payment from a customer. Once the customer clicks Continue to complete their payment, they are returned to your server and will be shown your customized checkout success page:

The story is not quite finished yet; you, as the receiver of funds, still need to accept payments made. Should you choose to accept the payments, then the following note will be added to the order:

Date Added	Customer Notified	Status	Comments
08/17/2005 15:29:38	✓	Preparing [PayPal IPN]	
08/17/2005 15:31:19	✓	Preparing [PayPal IPN]	
08/17/2005 15:34:11	✗	Processing	PayPal IPN Completed 27.99USD. David Mercer davidm@contechst.com is unverified. [Fee=USD Payment=instant Date=06:31:15 Aug 17, 2005 PDT ID=19C45404318674231]

Notice that at the bottom of the list we now have the latest record (in this case at 15:34:11): the customer hasn't been notified of this development by osCommerce (but remember that PayPal will notify them that their payment has been accepted), the Status of the order has been set to Processing as expected, but the really interesting point is that the Comments section is telling us that the actual process is Completed as opposed to Unfinished as it was initially. This means we have the money, safe and sound.

For the demo site, things were set up like this because we want the opportunity to print out an invoice and packing slip, and then finally set the status of the order to Delivered manually so that the final order page looks like this (note that we also emailed the customer to inform them of the delivery and they can now check the site to view the full order history of this order):

Date Added	Customer Notified	Status	Comments
08/17/2005 15:29:38	✓	Preparing [PayPal IPN]	
08/17/2005 15:31:19	✓	Preparing [PayPal IPN]	
08/17/2005 15:34:11	✗	Processing	PayPal IPN Completed 27.99USD. David Mercer davidm@contechst.com is unverified. [Fee=USD Payment=instant Date=06:31:15 Aug 17, 2005 PDT ID=19C45404318674231]
08/17/2005 16:00:46	✓	Delivered	

Obviously, how you choose to deal with your particular setup will come from what you want out of the site and what you learn as you go along. Having been through this example, though, you should feel pretty good about the process of obtaining payments via PayPal. Of course, there is plenty of testing to do, and you should always ensure that your purchases and stock levels are adjusted as you expect—you can take a look at the Products Purchased report in the admin tool to confirm whether the correct products have indeed been purchased by your PayPal customer.

There is really no substitute for the two things to ensure you have everything set up correctly: practice and experience. Make sure you play around with every aspect of this module so that you understand how it works thoroughly. Then, how to best implement the functionality can be tweaked as you gain experience—you may wish to do things entirely differently altogether.

For example, you may wish to entice customers to actually click on the Continue button when finished with PayPal so that they do go back to your site and are given a confirmation email, instead of logging off and then wondering why no one is talking to them. For this, open up the includes/modules/payments/paypal_ipn.php file and search for the following two lines somewhere about line 330:

```
$parameters['cancel_return'] = tep_href_link(FILENAME_CHECKOUT_PAYMENT, '',
'SSL');
$parameters['bn'] = $this->identifier;
```

Under that line, add the following line so your code looks like this:

```
$parameters['cancel_return'] = tep_href_link(FILENAME_CHECKOUT_PAYMENT, '',
'SSL');
$parameters['bn'] = $this->identifier;
$parameters['cbt'] = 'Click here for email confirmation of your order';
```

Once you have saved that, take a look at the button you get when you are making payments via PayPal. You should see something like the following:

Pretty neat, huh? Apart from this, the other important thing we learned in this section is that we can create custom order statuses to suit our needs in the Localization section of the admin tool. In this case, we set the status to Processing once we were in a position to accept funds. As you will see in Chapter 7, when we deal with the download controller, having a solid approach to naming the various statuses your store encounters is quite important.

That about wraps it up for a live, functional PayPal-based payment system, but you should never leave things as they are. You need to secure everything using encryption, and for this you will probably need access to some sort of certificate and key generation tool or be able to use a secure server—most good web hosts should provide you with either.

Credit Card Payments

Let's begin this section by stating that there are several caveats to consider when embarking on the journey to credit card payment bliss! The main one is that it can be quite a pain in the proverbial back end of your application getting an Internet Merchant Account. This is because Internet transactions are considered to be at a high risk from fraud, and one result is that transaction fees are often higher too. There is not really much help that this book can offer you in terms of obtaining a merchant account—this is between you and your bank or merchant account provider.

For more information on obtaining merchant accounts, visit the service providers of your choice, who will have plenty of information about how to use them and how to find your way around the system in general. For example, all the following sites will furnish you with plenty of relevant information to help you make your choice:

- `http://www.authorizenet.com/solutions/merchantsolutions/onlinemerchant account/`
- `http://www.secpay.com/`
- `http://www.psigate.com/merchantaccount.asp`

Secondly, you need to make absolutely certain that you are not providing a platform for hackers to gain access to customer's credit information by not implementing proper security over the entire site. If we were to accept credit card details with the site in its current form, we would certainly be deserving of the term *negligent* in our responsibility to protect client's information, because there is no secure method of information exchange between the clients, us, and the financial institutions that we need to interact with.

> While we are setting up payments using credit cards here, you should not consider the job complete until you have implemented security for the payments, which is discussed in the following chapter.

Cheer up, though; it's not all doom and gloom. Apart from what has just been mentioned, the process of getting set up is much the same as it was for PayPal. Before we go any further it might be worthwhile to lay out all the players in the credit card transaction world so that you have a fair idea of what you need to do to get things working:

- **Merchant Account**: Anyone who wants to process credit card payments themselves (as opposed to letting PayPal handle it) will need a merchant account. Further, if you want to provide online payment facilities, you will need an Internet merchant account, and not your run-of-the-mill account. For some businesses it is particularly difficult to obtain a merchant account—however, so long as you stick to retailing fairly tangible goods you should be safe in this respect. Anything that leaves a verifiable trail comes in handy as proof should the question of fraud arise.

- **Acquirers**: Any institutions that issue merchant accounts, often banks, are known as acquirers. For example, HSBC and Barclays are two well known acquiring banks.

- **Payment Service Provider**: These companies, among other things, have as their main focus the task of facilitating payment transactions for merchants (such as yourself) via a payment gateway.

You might find that depending on whom you work with, your acquirer offers full support for your payments transactions, in which case you may not need a payment service provider. Of course, most of the payment modules available are for use by payment service providers, and not the banks directly.

> Having set up PayPal facilities, customers are already able to pay with their credit cards or bank accounts. Adding credit card facilities here is really an exercise in making non-PayPal customers' lives easier.

So, the process is still the same as it was for PayPal:

1. Sign up with the relevant corporations to obtain a merchant account or a payment gateway.
2. Install the relevant module.
3. Test, test, and test again.
4. Rake in the cash.

Accordingly, there isn't too much to discuss by way of anything new here other than to show a couple of examples in action. We will begin with the Credit Card module and also demonstrate the PsiGate payment module.

The Credit Card Module

You can make use of the Credit Card module to process payments manually if you have a merchant account. Basically, the details that are provided on the site by the customer are simply stored in the database, ready for you to process them accordingly. On the surface of things, this seems like a really nice and easy way to do things, but don't be fooled, you can get yourself into a lot of trouble doing things this way. Let's look at how everything works so that it is clearer.

Head on over to your admin tool, and click on install for the Credit Card module and enable the module by setting the first option to True so that your page looks like this:

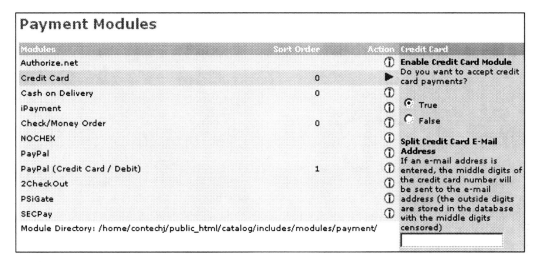

Update that, and head on to the site and make a purchase. When you get to the checkout-payment page, you should now have the option to receive credit card payments; enter the dummy credit card value and add a date later than the current one as the expiry time, like so:

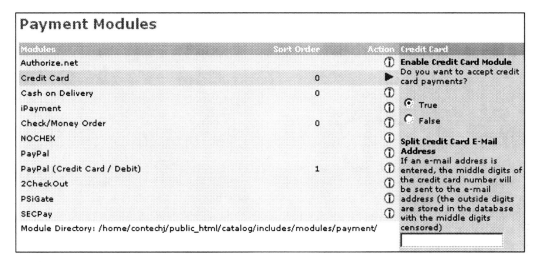

Carry on with the purchase until you receive the checkout success page, and then go to the Orders section of the admin tool and take a look at the information given for this latest purchase. You should have something that looks a lot like this:

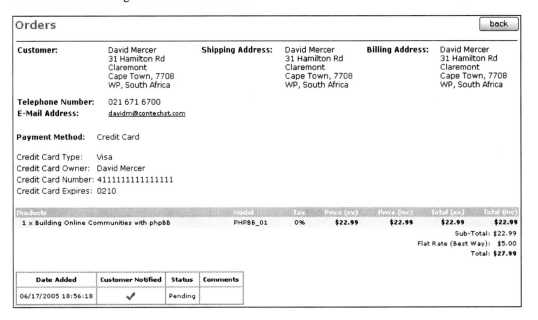

A sight like this will generally have your average security expert in tears because not only are we storing the customer's credit card information in our database, but we are also allowing access to that information bundled up and presented in a nice report format. If anyone ever gained access to the admin tool, they would be able to read off client credit card information from here. Even worse, if a hacker ever gained access to the database, they would now be able to read off all the credit card information directly from the database.

"Sure, but this will all eventually be password protected, and we will be adding security later" I hear you say. Well, actually this very module comes with a bit more security, so let's try that out. Go back to the payment module's edit page and add in an email address to which you would like half of the credit information sent. Save that and repeat the process and notice that this time the order page looks like this:

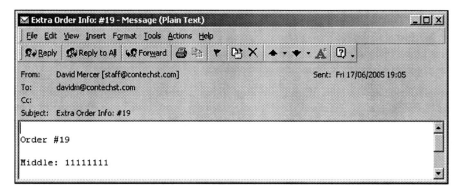

Well, that's slightly better because now if someone gained access to the site, he or she would only be able to get their hands on half of credit card info; the other half is not held on the site. Instead, it has been sent via email to the address you specified:

Now you can simply match the middle numbers to the outer numbers via the order number, which is common to both records, and are thereby able to retain the complete details without running the risk of holding all the information in one place. While this is much better, it is still exceptionally poor in terms of the type of security you should be hoping to implement, because that email has been sent to you in a non-secure manner.

Assuming someone knows that this is going on, they could intercept the unencrypted message and match the numbers up. This might all seem like quite a reasonable risk to take, but bear in mind what is at stake—your livelihood. If customers find out that your site, and therefore their private financial data, has been compromised (and they will because they will notice fraudulent transactions on their accounts), then as a business, your reputation is more or less irrevocably destroyed.

While you could always take the information and encrypt it before emailing it to yourself, you will still have to work with this information, and somewhere along the line there will be a chink in the armor. Rather don't take the risk at all, and let someone else handle it—there are plenty of reputable businesses who plow far more resources than you or I could into making their services secure, so that you can use them. It may hurt to fork out for the service, but it's nothing compared to the trouble you could land yourself in.

Having seen how the Credit Card module works, let's move on to look at how one of the service-provider modules functions.

The PsiGate Module

It's important to bear in mind before we test this module that each gateway service might have a slightly different methodology for processing credit card payments. For example, those of you who try SECPay will notice that at no time does the customer enter credit card details onto the merchant's site—instead, the browser is redirected to a secure payment page on the SECPay server, before being returned to the merchant site once the payment details have been entered.

> Whatever module you choose to use, or even if you choose to write your own application code to handle payments, setting everything up is really all about learning how your gateway service operates and using that knowledge to integrate its service into your application.

PsiGate makes it easy for us to test our application because we can run test values off it without having to register with it first. Consequently, pretty much the only thing you need to do is install the module in the Payments section as you have seen in previous examples, navigate to the payments page on your site, and run through the payment process as normal.

The astute observer will notice a slight difference in the processing of payments once the PsiGate option has been checked. Let's run through that quickly because it will also illustrate the generic process followed by all the other gateway services (more or less). Suppose you have entered the relevant test info into your site, so that your page looks like this:

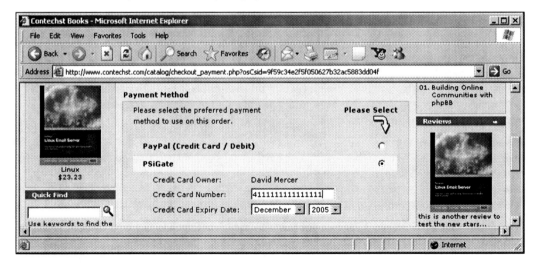

Click on Continue to get to the order confirmation page. This is where things change a bit behind the scenes. Once the customer confirms his or her details are all correct and clicks on Continue, that information is sent to a secure PsiGate server instead of simply being held on your site. You can view the status bar in your browser immediately after clicking on Continue to confirm this, and can also see a quick notice from the actual PsiGate site before it redirects the customer back to your store, like so:

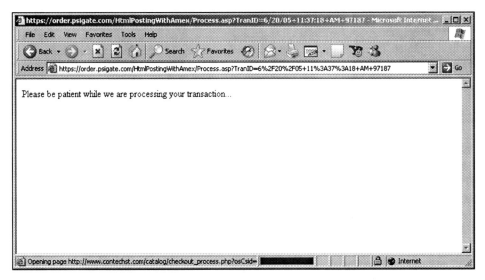

Notice from this screenshot that we are actually executing the Process.asp page on the https://order.psigate.com/ URL, and the target URL, shown in the Status bar at the bottom of the screen is the checkout_process.php page back on the store's server. As well as this, the session is preserved because the target also includes the session ID parameter (not quite visible).

So, what has happened here is that your store's server has sent information to the PsiGate secure server, which has processed the information and returned its results. If the transaction has been successful, the customer sees the usual Your Order has been Processed message on the checkout success page (or whatever your equivalent of this is). If the order is not successful, then the error is collected by the payment module and outputted to the customer's screen.

So what type of options do we have to work with? Well, as we showed for the PayPal section, here is a table representing all the options and their values and meanings:

Property	Setting
Enable PSiGate Module Do you want to accept PSiGate payments?	Obviously this is set to True if you want customers to be able to use this form of payment.
Merchant ID Merchant ID used for the PSiGate service	This ID will be assigned to you once you have an internet merchant account. Please see the PsiGate site for more info on this: http://www.psigate.com/faq.asp.

Property	Setting
Transaction Mode Transaction mode to use for the PSiGate service	The first value, Production, should be enabled once you decide to go live. The three that follow are used for testing purposes to ensure your system is behaving correctly. For example, select Always Good to test for successful transactions while testing.
Transaction Type Transaction type to use for the PSiGate service	Setting this to Sale means that PsiGate will treat this as a normal transaction and transfer funds appropriately—use this only if the product reaches the client immediately (in other words, the product is downloadable). PreAuth will ensure the funds are available (reserved), but will not perform the transaction—this is left for you to do manually from your PsiGate Admin section once you have delivered the product. Use PostAuth if you want to settle a PreAuth transaction which reserves funds. You must have the PreAuth order ID and the correct amount to do this—for more info see the PsiGate docs at www.psigate.com/java.pdf.
Credit Card Collection Should the credit card details be collected locally or remotely at PSiGate?	You can choose whether customers will enter their credit card information onto your site or onto PsiGate's site. If in doubt, take the responsibility off your hands and pass the buck to PsiGate.
Transaction Currency The currency to use for credit card transactions	The only two options for this module are Canadian dollars and US dollars since PsiGate only deals with these two currencies.
Payment Zone If a zone is selected, only enable this payment method for that zone.	Once again, you should select the zones you wish this module to be enabled for. For example, you may prefer to use PsiGate in North America, but SECPay in Europe.
Set Order Status Set the value for the status of orders made with this payment module	You can set this to whatever value option you like; however, remember to be consistent in your choice of status because you may wish to programmatically implement features based on the Status of payments at some stage. For example Preparing [PayPal IPN] is not a bright choice because this has nothing to do with PsiGate.
Sort order of display. Sort order of display. Lowest is displayed first.	As usual, you can select the order of appearance using this option.

There are, of course, many other modules that you may opt to use depending on your business's needs and setup. The exact manner in which the module implements the payments is really dependent on the gateway that you are using, but what you have seen here is a good outline of what is expected once you have an internet merchant account against which to run e-commerce transactions.

One final thought before we move on. If you are concerned about the safety of your business and wish to know more about how to prevent or reduce fraud, then visit your payment service provider or acquirer online and look over their fraud-detection software or other such products. With that out of the way, we should briefly look at a few more methods of payment, which might come in handy somewhere along the line.

Alternative Forms of Payments

While credit cards and PayPal payments are probably the easiest and most convenient for a customer to use, not everyone will trust the Internet with their payment details and will instead prefer to use more old-fashioned methods. Ironically, a higher percentage of fraud is associated with check payments than with credit cards from online sales, but there you go.

Be careful with checks and money orders. Some banks will clear the funds in your account immediately when you deposit a check into your account. Acting on good faith, you then promptly deliver the product, only to find that the bank has removed the funds from your account once the check bounced and the customer has either maliciously or unwittingly left you out of pocket. Ouch!!

If you feel that your sales will be adversely affected due to the lack of other payment methods, then by all means, read on…

Checks and Money Orders

This module is about as easy as it comes to set up. Simply go along to the Payments section and click install. Then, edit it appropriately (the settings are self explanatory, or have already been covered several times), and away you go. Obviously, you would not change the status of the order until you received the check or the money order, and you certainly would not want to release your products or make them available till you are in possession of the funds.

Another issue you will need to research is whether or not the form of payment is valid for you. Money orders may not be redeemable if you are not based in the US. Apart from doing a bit of background research on the niceties of each form of payment, there are no real concerns about security on the site because no sensitive information is passed between the customer and the store. This makes it easy for you to implement, but an exercise in patience for the customer as they wait for you to receive and process the payments.

Cash on Delivery

If you are going to be delivering the products you sell, then the Cash on Delivery module is probably worth installing. Again, there is nothing complex about this module, and editing should present no problem for you. The only things worth mentioning here are that:

- The chances being fairly high that you only deliver within a single zone, the Payment Zone option becomes far more important because you can enable this option for only your locality.
- Merchants can ship CoD using UPS, but there are extra costs involved. See the UPS site at http://www.ups.com for more details.

Shipping

There are six shipping modules currently shipped with osCommerce by default, which give you a fair amount of control over how you handle the delivery of your goods. There are also a huge number of modules available that can augment the default functionality, or provide new facilities altogether. The best thing to do when organizing your site's shipping is to sit back and think carefully about who will be buying what, and where they are likely to be.

Once you have a good idea about where most of your products are going, you can develop a shipping strategy to suit your needs. For example, if you are only going to be shipping to a relatively small geographical area, and your products are more or less the same in terms of size and weight, then a flat shipping rate may be appropriate. However, it is more than likely that you will want a more fine-grained level of control over your shipping charges, so let's take a quick look through the modules that are available (excluding the flat-rate module, which is trivial to install).

Before we do this, though, I should point out that while it is pretty simple to install and control each individual shipping module, it is not so easy to actually obtain precisely what you want in terms of shipping charges. What I mean by this is that you could decide to offer several methods of shipping based on the various locations and zones you are retailing to. If you do this, then you have to ensure that each one will cover your shipping costs wherever the customer is based (or is disabled if that option is not viable).

In other words, a flat rate will always be a set value even if someone is purchasing from overseas, and the customer will more than likely choose the cheapest option available regardless of whether you meant them to choose one option or the other. So be careful you don't end up with a situation where the customer is offered several shipping options, one of which is not enough to cover the shipping costs.

Flat Rates

Having said this, you can use flat rates for several different zones, so don't feel you are restricted to only implementing flat rates to one area. To do this, make copies of the flat.php file in the includes/modules/shipping/ and includes/languages/english/modules/shipping/ folders. Then edit these copies, replacing each occurrence of the term flat or FLAT with the name of the copied files. For example, I have named the new files flat1.php in both folders, and replaced each occurrence of the term flat or FLAT with flat1 or FLAT1—a simple search and replace will work here. The result is a new flat-rate module, which can be used to ship flat rates to a different zone.

This is incredibly useful if you want to make flat rates to specific countries without having to bother with zone-rate settings or other forms of shipping. Looking at the shipping options available on the demo store, you can see the following:

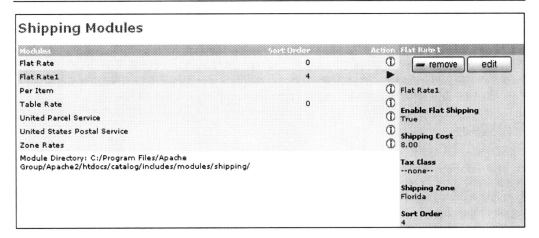

It's clear that we now have two flat-rate modules, with the new one only being enabled for the Florida shipping zone, with a slightly higher Shipping Cost to distinguish it from the original flat rate module. Looking at the effect this has on customers who are based in Florida (shown in the following screenshot), we can see that they now have two flat-rate options available (obviously you would only want one rate enabled per zone, but this is left as is to demonstrate the point):

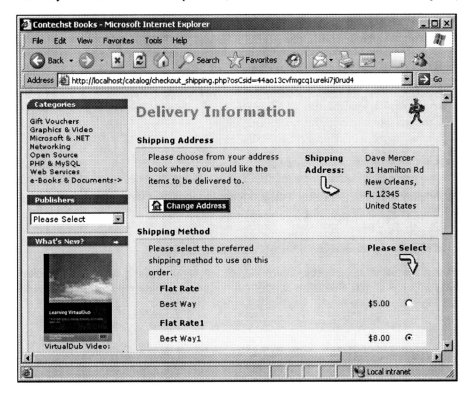

Now, you will probably want to make your new flat-rate modules display more descriptive names such as Flat Rate to Europe or Flat Rate to Australia, and you will need to test to ensure that customers from certain zones, or goods that belong to a certain tax class, get linked to the correct flat-rate shipping method. However, we won't dwell on this any more because you should be able to add as many flat-rate modules (or any other module for that matter) as you like, given what you have just seen here. Just play around and experiment to find what works for you…

Per Item

Once again, this is pretty straightforward. Simply install the module and away you go! osCommerce will multiply the number of items in the customer's shopping cart on checkout and will deliver a total based on that alone. You can set the Shipping Cost you wish to charge per item, as well as a Handling Fee, Tax Class, Shipping Fee, and Sort Order. Of interest here is the handling fee, which applies to all the shipping modules. Adding an amount here allows you to cover other costs such as packaging material and labor, by tacking that amount onto the shipping price.

Of course, this option is probably not ideal if you are selling large number of products per purchase, and packaging them up in one container. Obviously, you need to always think of the most efficient and cost effective way to ship your products so that you can pass those savings on to your customers.

Table Rate

This option gives a lot more control over how you make your charges, through the use of a shipping table. There are two module-specific options here, which you will need to get used to in order to effectively utilize this form of payment.

- Shipping Table: This option determines the total shipping cost based on the total cost or weight of items. You can set the charges using a colon- and comma-delimited list as shown here:

  25:8.50,50:5.50,100:3.50,500:1.50

  This will cause osCommerce to add a charge of $8.50 for the first 25 units of product (units precede the colon, which is followed by the price), from there to 50 units, we charge $5.50, from 50 to 100 units we charge $3.50, and from 100 to 500 we charge only $1.50.

- Table Method: This allows you to select whether osCommerce should base its calculations on the weight of the products or the total cost.

That's all well and good so far; we have now looked at several shipping methods that we can offer to customers. However, to reiterate the idea that you need to carefully control where each module is enabled, the following screenshot highlights a couple of points:

In this figure, there are two options offered to the customer. Now, it is clear that the customer is going for the cheaper option, which is based on the table rate with the Table Method of the Table Rates option, set to Price, defined such that any purchase over $50 gets delivered free. The Per Item option simply adds $2.50 to the delivery price for every item purchased, so it increases while the other decreases.

The unfortunate thing about both these Shipping Methods is that the Shipping Address is in Africa, and will likely cost Contechst Books a lot more to ship than either quote, assuming Contechst is based in the States.

> Remember that you can enable free shipping for purchases over a certain value by defining this value in the Shipping section of the Order Total Module page (found below Shipping in the Modules category).

It is recommended that you play around with the settings in the Order Total Modules section in order to get a good idea of what functionality it provides. Since it is fairly straightforward, we won't cover it all here, and it is left to you as an exercise to familiarize yourself with the various options.

UPS and USPS

As with the PayPal and credit card modules, you will need to obtain an account with these two service providers before you can go ahead and offer this shipping option—or at least make contact with the provider of the service to confirm orders. Let's begin with UPS…

The big advantage of using UPS is that they are extremely convenient for you, as the business owner, and the customer alike. They, like other large shipping businesses, pride themselves on their reliability and are certainly justified in doing so. If you enable this module, then using the shipping address you entered in the Configuration section, the payment module contacts the UPS server to obtain a quote for the price of the delivery, and will present all the different relevant options available for the customer to choose from.

Using a service like this takes the responsibility out of your hands because it becomes the responsibility of the shipper to live up to their promises. For example, suppose you were based in the States and a purchase was made on your store from somewhere else in the world. Instead of having to work with a combination of complicated shipping rates, UPS would simply give you its worldwide quote, like so:

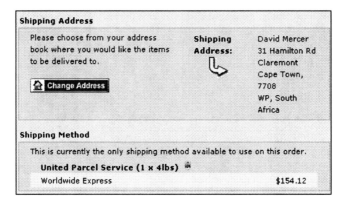

Now, when the customer recoils in horror at the price of delivery, they may decide to provide a shipping address in the US where they can pick up the product during their upcoming visit (for sake of argument). In this case, UPS will use its table rates to calculate the cost and present its different options, like this:

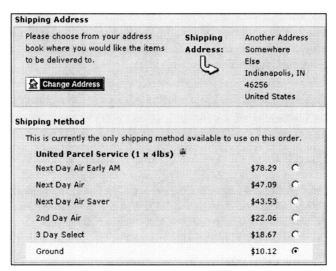

This is obviously extremely convenient for everyone concerned because the only thing left for you to do (assuming the customer decides to use UPS) is get in touch with them to confirm this shipping—ideally, you would get an account with UPS so that you can automate pick up along with a host of other advantages.

Before we leave UPS, you should also take a quick look over the editable options for this module to decide on the method of pick up, whether you want to package products yourself or leave it to UPS to provide material, or whether you are delivering to a residential or commercial address. Of course, UPS itself can help you make these decisions if you register with them or look up their site at `http://www.ups.com`.

So, what's the disadvantage? Well, let's face it; you could probably get products to your customers a little cheaper... enough said!

USPS does things slightly differently in that you need to register with them before you can use their servers to automate the shipping process. You can visit them at `http://www.uspsprioritymail.com/et_regcert.html` in order to find out more about this service. Below is an excerpt from the registration confirmation email, which explains how the service is used:

> *Your Web Tools User ID and Password to integrate USPS Web Tools are provided above. The User ID and Password are used for testing your implementation of the Web Tools. With these, you may begin sending calls to the test server. The address to the test server is: testing.shippingapis.com and the path is /ShippingAPITest.dll. Use this information in combination with your User ID, Password and your XML string to send a request to the USPS servers. For more details, refer to the programming guides (located at www.usps.com/webtools) for the specific API you are integrating.*

> *A sample test request would look like:*
> *"http://testing.shippingapis.com/ShippingAPITest.dll?*
> *API=[API_Name]&XML=[XML_String_containing_User_ID_and_Password]"*

> *When you have completed your testing, email the USPS Internet Customer Care Center (ICCC). They will switch your profile to allow you access to the production server and will provide you with the production URL.*

Of course, this serves to outline how the service works, but this complexity is hidden from us because osCommerce takes care of all this for us. For example, you can confirm that osCommerce is querying the correct server by inspecting the `usps.php` file in the `includes/modules/shipping` folder:

```
switch (MODULE_SHIPPING_USPS_SERVER) {
    case 'production': $usps_server = 'production.shippingapis.com';
                       $api_dll = 'shippingapi.dll';
                       break;
    case 'test':
    default:           $usps_server = 'testing.shippingapis.com';
                       $api_dll = 'ShippingAPITest.dll';
                       break;
}
```

From this you can see that the correct server and DLL are targeted by osCommerce. Getting everything working is simply a case of inserting your username and password into the module in the admin tool as well as making a few other standard decisions, which are common to all shipping modules.

Zone Rates

This module is quite interesting in that you can select the price of shipping to a specific zone and for specified package weights. The problem is that this is limited to only one zone at the moment, and so is not effective for anything outside that zone. The following screenshot shows the results of using this module when a customer based outside the US makes a purchase:

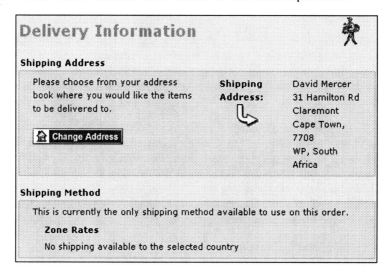

Hmm, none of these options are really ideal by themselves, so what is the solution? The smart money is on a combination of the different modules using zones to enable or disable them. Of course, this won't quite get us to where we want to be in the case of the demo site, because this is a truly global English-language technical bookstore. Let's take a look at that now…

Contechst Book's Shipping Solution

The majority of Contechst Books' sales come from the United States, so we would like to offer an excellent shipping service, with a variety of options to cater for customers who might be willing to pay the extra amount to have their books delivered ASAP. Accordingly, we will use the UPS module to cater to the national market. However, not everyone in the US might want to pay the slightly higher prices of UPS and may be happy for the package to make its way a little slower but proportionally cheaper. So we need another option to cater for these people—it's easy enough to enable the Table Rate payment module for only the US, so that is what we'll do.

While most of the sales come from the States, areas like Europe, Africa, India, and Australia are also appreciable markets that need to be catered for in our shipping plan. Accordingly, the second shipping method we will make available is the Zone Rates shipping module. But we are still limited to specifying only one zone, which is not sufficient if we want to deliver all over the world, so we need to make a slight modification to the code in order to get the module to allow as many zones as we need.

In the `public_html/catalog/includes/modules/shipping/zones.php` file, you can simply modify the line that reads:

```
$this->num_zones = 1;
```

to something like this (depending on how many zones you need):

```
$this->num_zones = 4;
```

Now, of course, comes the slightly tricky bit. In order for the new settings to take effect properly, you need to reinstall the module. If you reinstall the module, you will lose all your current settings, so remember to make backups of whatever info you need before doing this. Now, when you access the module again, you get something like the following:

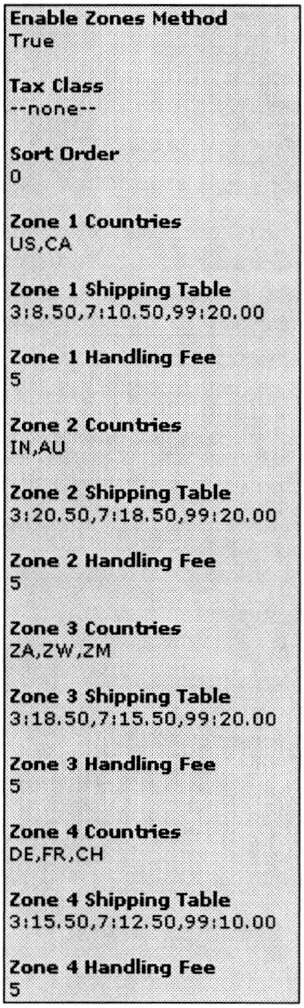

Enable Zones Method
True

Tax Class
--none--

Sort Order
0

Zone 1 Countries
US,CA

Zone 1 Shipping Table
3:8.50,7:10.50,99:20.00

Zone 1 Handling Fee
5

Zone 2 Countries
IN,AU

Zone 2 Shipping Table
3:20.50,7:18.50,99:20.00

Zone 2 Handling Fee
5

Zone 3 Countries
ZA,ZW,ZM

Zone 3 Shipping Table
3:18.50,7:15.50,99:20.00

Zone 3 Handling Fee
5

Zone 4 Countries
DE,FR,CH

Zone 4 Shipping Table
3:15.50,7:12.50,99:10.00

Zone 4 Handling Fee
5

OK, so the rates aren't too important for us since this is just a demo, but we have a pretty authoritative shipping policy in place, which you can observe by viewing the options presented to customers coming from different areas around the world. So, as we expect (and require), a customer purchasing from Africa has two options available to them—UPS and Zone Rate, which offer different pricing based on how fast they are going to arrive:

Notice that these customers aren't offered table rates, which apply only to the States, and that they aren't offered UPS's specialized quotes for US-based customers, which is just fine. Don't worry about the actual numbers involved for now; you will need to work out what is appropriate for you on the basis of your business model and specific costs. To round this off, the following screenshot shows the options available to a US-based customer:

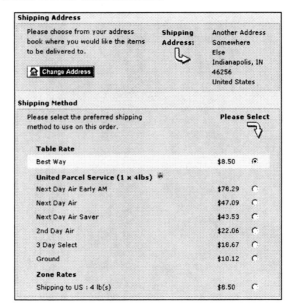

Now you can see why a combination of shipping options is the best solution, because just as we desired, US customers can choose to use UPS, but now they are also offered the table rate, which is slightly cheaper because we are sending it to them directly ourselves.

Notice that there is a Zone Rates option given here, which is the same price as the Table Rates. These values would diverge if, for example, the zone changed, or the weight of the products changed, but this is not really a concern because the Zone Rates module is used mainly for pricing overseas shipping. If you feel it would be wiser not to offer all three options for US customers, then you could simply enable the Zone Rates module for only those overseas areas that you ship to. This would then provide UPS or Table Rates only to US customers.

Summary

Having a comprehensive payment and shipment policy goes a long way to running a successful online business. After completing this chapter, you should now know exactly what you need to do in order to implement your own store's payment and shipping functionality. Hopefully, you will have decided to take as little risk as possible by handing over your customer's credit information to secure and trusted providers. I should reiterate the fact that you should only use trusted payment service providers—there are a lot of fraudsters out there.

So, by this stage you should have all your payment facilities up and running, with all the requisite accounts working as they should. Further, your calculations of the price of goods should include shipping options with the correct values for your target customers. But the job is not done yet. Recall that we are communicating with PayPal's IPN server without the use of encryption. Even worse, we have not secured any part of the site yet—it is wholly possible that a hacker could gain control of your entire site without too much trouble.

Remember to comprehensively test every conceivable permutation of payments, incorrect payments, shipping details, incorrect addresses, and so on before you consider your payments and shipping to be robust enough to take to the live site.

7
More Advanced Topics

By and large, you should find that you can now work fairly confidently with your osCommerce application. There are, of course, plenty of new things still to be learned and some of them are actually quite important to the safety and well being of your site and business. Not everything is quite so critical, and there a re a few things you might want to learn in order to make your life easier, or even just to spruce up your site a bit.

Accordingly, this chapter presents a kind of grab bag of different topics, which you will no doubt find a use for in the time to come. Specifically, we will:

- Begin by taking a fairly in-depth look at securing the admin tool as well as securing payments
- See how to use a community contribution to provide a new type of report
- Use a community contribution to properly control the purchasing and delivery of downloadable products
- Briefly discuss how to make cool button templates for use throughout your site
- Learn some of the insiders' secrets for Search Engine Optimization

Hopefully, by the end of this chapter you will know enough to make you feel confident about the stability, reliability, and future of your online business. After working with osCommerce for some time you will probably find that you have outgrown the advice given in this text and wish to start creating your own additions by writing PHP add-ons or modifying the source code yourself. If that's the case, consider looking at the professional version of this book for more information.

For now though, let's get on with the last few topics before you start retailing for real...

Securing the Administration Tool

Without a doubt, one of the major potential security threats comes from using the administration tool over the Internet. Should someone gain access to this tool on your live site, they could cause untold mischief, and much wailing and gnashing of teeth will ensue. As a result, we are going to enforce the use of a username and password in order to gain access to the admin folder, as well as ensure that the admin folder is only available over a secure server (which uses SSL to encrypt communications).

> You might also wish to change the name of the admin folder to something random, which will add a small amount of security in that it may not be immediately obvious to a potential hacker where this web-based tool is housed. If you do so you will need to edit `config.php` to reflect these changes as none of your file paths should contain the word admin anymore.

Before we do go ahead and secure the admin tool, it is worth considering that forcing communications over HTTPS will slow down whatever interaction we have with the server. It's a trade-off; if you don't think it is necessary to use SSL for communication with your server, then perhaps simply implement password security—but be warned that it is possible to intercept passwords that aren't transmitted in encrypted form, or over SSL.

Creating Password-Protected Folders

The first thing you should do is check your hosting package to see what facilities it has in place in order to password protect your files. More than likely you will simply be given something like a Web Protect option:

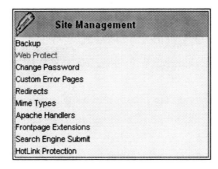

In this case, after selecting this option, the following page is presented:

As you can see, all that is required is to check the box at the top left, and add as many new users as you wish to have access to that folder. Bear in mind that you should only create as many accounts as are absolutely necessary (preferably only one) and no more. Having unused accounts lying around is poor security practice. That's nice and easy to do, but what happens if you don't have access to this kind of functionality?

In order to enforce the use of a password on a certain folder, you will need to make use of the .htaccess file. This is either present by default or, if it is not, you will need to create a blank text file called .htaccess (with no other extensions) and place it in the admin folder. Now, there are a few things you need to note with regards to the use of .htaccess:

- .htaccess is for use by Apache, not PHP or IIS or anything else.

- .htaccess will influence the security of all subfolders below the folder it is present in, unless there is another .htaccess file in the subfolder. In this way you can secure an entire directory in one go, or give each subdirectory its own fine-grained security.

- You need to make sure that you can either use this method of securing files, or can make use of the native security system provided by your host.

- .htaccess commands are one line only. Make sure you use a new line for each separate command.

- Please make sure you set permissions on the .htaccess files correctly. If you make it readable by everyone, then your security is compromised. Set it to 644 so that the server can read it, but it is not readable by a browser.

Now, this really assumes that you will not have access to the Apache configuration file on your host's server, which is more than likely the case. Generally, you should only use .htaccess when you don't have access to the main configuration file (since this is where security should be implemented from) because using .htaccess slows down your site. That said, .htaccess should still give us enough security for our needs without being too much of a drag on performance, so let's continue.

The first thing you need to do is create a password file. You should leave this file out of your document root so that browsers cannot access it at all. You can simply create your own password file using the following format if you don't have access to the htpasswd utility:

```
username1:password1
username2:password2
...
```

Once this file is set up, you can refer to it in your .htaccess file as follows:

```
AuthType Basic
AuthName "Password Required"
AuthUserFile 'home\contechj\passwords\password'
Require user davidm
```

This tells Apache that the authentication type we are using is Basic, that the message to be displayed when requesting the username and password is Password Required, that the file to use to check the supplied credentials against is C:\Program Files\Apache Group\Apache2\passwords\password, and that the user we want is davidm.

Now, for either the Web Protect or .htaccess methods, if everything checks out, then each time you access the admin folder, you get prompted for a username and password, like so:

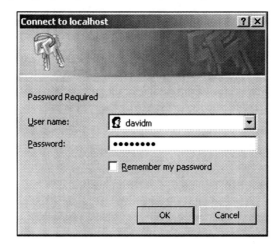

This is great! We now have a layer of security added to the site to protect the admin folder from a casual hack or two. Of course, we don't want these passwords submitted over the Internet without using a secure connection, so now we need to ensure that the admin folder is only available over SSL.

Implementing SSL for the admin Folder

The first step is to find out what SSL facilities are available to you on your live site and how you as the host's client can make use of them. Once you have established that, it should generally be a simple case of implementing that functionality—your service provider will often make this as easy as possible for you, and nine times out of ten it is simply a case of handing over the cash and having SSL enabled for your domain. Be advised that you will more than likely have to pay extra for this facility (and sometimes for extra certificates and so on) but given what you stand to lose if you don't make use of it, the expense is more than justified.

The host for Contechst Books simply enabled SSL, and all that was required was a couple of modifications to the .htaccess file in the admin folder and to the configure.php file in the admin/includes/ folder. More than likely this is all you will need to do as well, but it is possible that you need to move the admin tool to a secure folder—if this is the case, ensure that you make the necessary modifications to the file paths in the configure.php script. Assuming you need not do this, open up .htaccess in the admin folder and add the following line at the top, like so:

```
SSLRequireSSL

AuthType Basic
AuthName "Admin Tool"
AuthUserFile "path to your password file"
require valid-user
```

This forces the use of a secure server in order to access the folder and its contents. If you now try access the non-secure version—in this case, http://www.contechst.com/catalog/admin—you will get a message like the following:

This, of course, is very good news because we haven't even been prompted for a username and password. Now, it is possible to add a few lines to .htaccess to redirect the browser to a different page instead of simply showing this message, but since we are only securing the admin tool, and since we are only doing it for ourselves because we are the only ones who will access it, this is fine as it is.

Before we check whether the secure site works as planned, edit the configure.php script in the admin/includes folder like so (obviously, substitute in the values that reflect your site's specifics):

```
define('HTTP_SERVER', 'https://www.contechst.com');
```

This means that instead of trying to access the non-secure URLs when the administrator clicks on a link, the secure site is requested instead. If this setting wasn't changed, then only the admin/index.php file would be accessed through https; everything after that would revert back to the normal server (which is fine provided you are sure there is no sensitive information being passed thereafter). Having done this, navigate to the secure version of your admin tool, supply your username and password, and then fool around with the links to ensure everything is done through SSL:

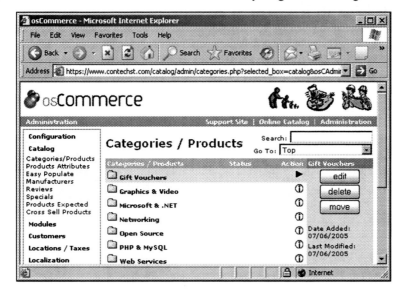

It's easy enough to ensure everything is working as planned! Simply check the URL of your page to verify it is being served by the secure server. If you really need proof, then copy one of the page's URLs into a new browser and attempt to access the page—you should notice that you are once again prompted for a password, regardless of the file you are trying to access. You may even want to make a couple of changes to check that uploading and downloading of information works.

It is quite likely that you have noticed a slight delay in the time it takes to serve pages now that we are using SSL and .htaccess. This is quite normal, and is the overhead you pay for adding security, because the server needs to do more work with each page it serves.

That's it! A major potential security hole has now been covered, and provided you use a sensible password (which uses both letters and numbers), you should be reasonably safe from intrusion with respect to the admin tool. There is still a fair way to go before we can breathe a sigh of relief that our store in general is safe—the next task is to use encryption to secure communications between the store's server and third parties, like PayPal.

Securing Payments

A close second in terms of importance is the ability to secure your payments. Why do I say a close second, instead of *the* highest importance? The answer is simply this: if you wanted to ensure your payments don't get hacked online, then you could always ask for bank transfers or some other offline form of payment, whereas there is no way you can maintain your site effectively without the use of some form of online admin tool.

The fundamental goal with respect to securing payments is to make the transmission of sensitive data (which occurs during the checkout stages of a purchase), as well as payment tracking after checkout using IPNs, undecipherable in the event that the transmission is intercepted. Luckily for us, this is the easiest thing in the world to do for the front end of the site, so let's take a look at that first.

The Front End of the Store

Simply open up the configure.php file in the catalog/includes/ folder and make the following SSL-related modifications (read: whatever is appropriate for your domain), if they have not already been set. (Please note that the comments accompanying HTTP_SERVER and HTTPS_SERVER have been moved to the next line for better readability):

```
// Define the webserver and path parameters
// * DIR_FS_* = Filesystem directories (local/physical)
// * DIR_WS_* = Webserver directories (virtual/URL)
   define('HTTP_SERVER', 'http://www.contechst.com');
// eg, http://localhost - should not be empty for productive servers
   define('HTTPS_SERVER', 'https://www.contechst.com');
// eg, https://localhost - should not be empty for productive servers
   define('ENABLE_SSL', 'true'); // secure webserver for checkout procedure?
   define('HTTP_COOKIE_DOMAIN', 'www.contechst.com');
   define('HTTPS_COOKIE_DOMAIN', 'www.contechst.com');
   define('HTTP_COOKIE_PATH', '/catalog/');
   define('HTTPS_COOKIE_PATH', '/catalog/');
   define('DIR_WS_HTTP_CATALOG', '/catalog/');
   define('DIR_WS_HTTPS_CATALOG', '/catalog/');
```

Of course, you need to make sure that these changes have taken effect as expected, so navigate to your store—take note of the URL:

Now try to log in using your customer account. Notice that you are immediately taken to the secure server in order to input your information—this means that customer usernames and logins are as secure as the customer decides to make them. In other words, they hopefully won't simply leave them lying around where someone can find them and use them:

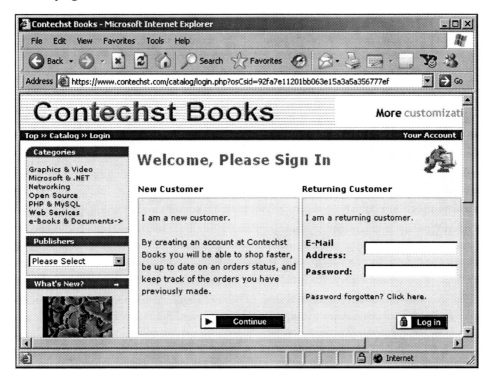

This is really great news for us because pretty much most of the work is done! If you are a new customer, then your registration (as well as your login, if you are a returning customer) takes place over SSL. Now, just because the login has taken place over SSL, doesn't mean the rest of the shopping needs to be done securely—in fact, we don't want it to be secure because it will slow down the site. The next time SSL comes into play is when the customer tries to make a purchase, or to view his or her account information.

What a pleasure! Everything is handled for us automatically by simply making a few settings in the configure.php file on an SSL-enabled site. Now, when a customer decides to check out, the HTTPS server is automatically used to ensure that communication between the browser and the store's server is secure. This is exactly what we required in our stated goals, and that's all that is needed on this side of things.

On the other side of the equation, not quite everything has been done.

The Back End of the Store

Knowing that a chain is only as strong as its weakest link, it should come as no surprise that we now have to look at the payment process behind the scenes in order to make absolutely certain that there is no chink in the armor, so to speak. This is where some knowledge of how your payment code is actually working comes in handy because knowing how something works will lend you some clues as to how to ensure it is secure. Let's begin with the PayPal module...

PayPal Payments

Having already installed the IPN PayPal module in the previous chapter, it is now time to look at how it goes about ensuring that communications between your store and the PayPal server are secure. A point to bear in mind is the following:

> If you have SSL enabled on your site, then you need not worry about encrypting IPN information, because osCommerce will ensure that your secure server is targeted by PayPal!

You can check up on this by looking at the line in your catalog/includes/modules/payment/paypal_ipn.php file, which reads something like:

```
$parameters['notify_url'] = tep_href_link('ipn.php', '', 'SSL', false, false);
```

This tells osCommerce to use SSL if it is enabled on your site, and assuming you have everything working correctly, it will dutifully use the secure server if it is available. If you still want to encrypt IPN communications, then there's quite a bit to do in order to ensure that PayPal and your server link up correctly, so the easiest thing to do is make a numbered list of tasks to follow, like so:

1. Make sure you have **OpenSSL** enabled on your website. If not, then you cannot use this module to encrypt your payment data using OpenSSL. We will discuss this situation at the end of this section.

2. Ensure your server has **cURL** installed. If not, your communications will not be sent using this method of transport and may even be sent as unencrypted information over a non-secure line.

3. Ensure your site has certificate and key generation tools. If not, ensure that you can obtain a private key and a public certificate.

4. Ensure that these keys and certificates are held outside the document root—otherwise you are asking for trouble.

5. Go to your PayPal account page and navigate to Encrypted Payment Settings under the Profile tab. If you don't have this option it may be because you are not yet Verified.

6. Download and save the PayPal Public Certificate to your `certificates` folder (or whatever it is called on your site) on your site's file system.

7. Add your public certificate to the PayPal site and obtain your unique ID.

Once this has all been done, you can now go to the administration tool and finish the settings on the PayPal IPN payment module. The table following shows you the settings used on the Contechst Books site, including a description of what each option does:

Property	Setting
Enable Encrypted Web Payments	Set this to True if you want data that is passed between your server and PayPal to be encrypted. Set this to False if you do not have access to OpenSSL on your site.
Your Private Key	Your path will be something like the following: `/home/contechstbooks/ssl/private/www.contechst.com.pem`. Ensure that this key is not held in the document root and is in .pem format.
Your Public Certificate	Your path will be something like the following: `/home/contechstbooks/ssl/certs/www.contechst.com.pem`. Ensure that this certificate is not held in the document root and is in .pem format.
PayPals Public Certificate	Save PayPal's certificate in your certificates folder like so: `/home/contechstbooks/ssl/certs/live_api.crt`
Your PayPal Public Certificate ID	Obtain this from the PayPal site once you have uploaded your certificate successfully.
Working Directory	The PayPal IPN module needs access to a temporary directory in order to work with files. Set this to be outside the document root: `/home/contechstbooks/tmp`
OpenSSL Location	The location of the OpenSSL binary file that can be used to sign and encrypt your information.

Naturally, you will need to test your site to ensure all this works correctly. However, if you do not have access to OpenSSL, then you will not be able to make use of encrypted payment notifications using this module. This is not cause for major concern provided you have the ability to use SSL. The reason for this is that the module has three different methods of operation as follows:

1. Use the `openssl_pkcs7_sign` and `openssl_pkcs7_encrypt` PHP functions to sign and encrypt information sent to the PayPal server.

2. Use the OpenSSL tool directly from an `exec` command to perform the same signing and encryption tasks as the previously mentioned PHP functions.

3. Send the information in unencrypted format.

Now, if you have Encrypted Web Payments enabled on your payment module's settings, then it will attempt to perform option 1, followed by option 2. If it is not possible to use OpenSSL and you have enabled this setting, it will kick up an error. If you disable this setting, then option 3 is performed.

It may seem on the surface of things that option 3 is not very secure, but recall that it can be just as secure as the first two options provided you are ensure PayPal is targeting a file on your secure server (HTTPS) for its IPN. If you have SSL enabled on your site, which you should have, then this file is only targeted over SSL (in other words, `https://www.contechst.com/ext/modules/payment/paypal_ipn/ipn.php` or `https://www.contechst.com/catalog/ipn.php`, depending on which version of the contribution you are using), which means that the information coming from PayPal is sent over SSL and is therefore secure.

If you do not have access to SSL, then unfortunately you will have to do without securing the back end of the PayPal payment module. Remember that this is not a train-smash—no credit card details are transferred between sites at any stage. The next section shows how information can be encrypted quite easily before being sent off by email. This could easily be adapted to encrypt whatever type of information you wish, so if you are feeling bold, perhaps you could try implementing your own secure transactions for your payment modules.

Credit Card Payments

There were two types of credit card payment that were discussed in the previous chapter. The first option, storing credit card details on your site, is really not recommended because it turns your store into a target for credit card fraud. That said, we should still take a look at this particular method to ensure that we can, as an exercise, ensure it is relatively secure—after all, any security practice is a good thing. Following that we will look at the PsiGate payment method to see if there is anything we can do to make this more secure.

Now, the first thing to do is look at the process of accepting credit card payments. For a start we already know that the front end of the store is secure because any checkout transactions are done over SSL, which includes the credit card payment methods. This means we can be fairly confident that the customer details will get to us unmolested.

We can now choose whether or not to email the middle digits of the number to a specified email address, or to keep the whole credit card number in the database. Following that, you would use an EFTPOS merchant account terminal, for example, and process the credit card details away from your store. That being the case, there are three areas of concern; specifically, hackers might:

1. Gain access to the administration tool and be able to view credit card details

2. Gain access to the database

3. Intercept emails

Point number 1 is no longer a concern since the administration tool is password protected and runs over a secure server. This is about as secure as we need it to be. This leaves points 2 and 3, of which the first will fall under a discussion on database security. So that leaves us with the final point to deal with now: what can be done to secure emails sent to us by our online store?

Well, let's take a look at the code that is used to send the email within the credit card payment module:

```
function after_process() {
    global $insert_id;

    if ( (defined('MODULE_PAYMENT_CC_EMAIL')) &&
         (tep_validate_email(MODULE_PAYMENT_CC_EMAIL)) ) {
        $message = 'Order #' . $insert_id . "\n\n" . 'Middle: ' .
        $this->cc_middle . "\n\n";

        tep_mail('', MODULE_PAYMENT_CC_EMAIL, 'Extra Order Info: #' .
        $insert_id, $message, STORE_OWNER, STORE_OWNER_EMAIL_ADDRESS);
    }
}
```

You will notice that the $message variable, which contains the middle digits, is simply sent as is with no encryption. Obviously, we would like to be able to encrypt that if at all possible. Of course, it is possible, and only takes a minute or so. For example, I have modified this function like so:

```
function after_process() {
    global $insert_id;

    if ( (defined('MODULE_PAYMENT_CC_EMAIL')) &&
         (tep_validate_email(MODULE_PAYMENT_CC_EMAIL)) ) {

        // Added mcrypt functionality to transmit the middle
        // digits of the credit card details in encrypted form.

        $message = 'Order #' . 'encrypted' . "\n\n" . 'Middle: ' .
        $this->cc_middle . "\n\n";
        $key = "Secret Key";
        $encrypted_data = base64_encode(mcrypt_encrypt(MCRYPT_3DES,
          $key, $message, MCRYPT_MODE_CBC));
        $message = $encrypted_data;

        tep_mail('', MODULE_PAYMENT_CC_EMAIL, 'Extra Order Info: #' .
          $insert_id, $message, STORE_OWNER, STORE_OWNER_EMAIL_ADDRESS);
    }
}
```

Now when you receive an email from an order you will get it in this form:

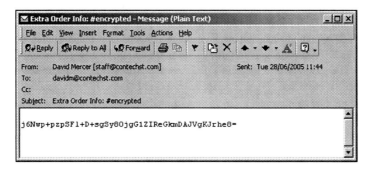

You can now decrypt this using your secret key value quite easily and match the values to the order number that is given in the Subject of the email. Note that there is no point in giving away any information if you are going to use encryption. Passing the order number as clear text gives a potential hacker a interesting piece of information, which is why we haven't done this.

It is quite possible that your host provides similar functionality, so check with your host if there is already something similar in place that you can use. If not, then you will have to install **MCrypt** on your machine—this can be obtained at `http://mcrypt.sourceforge.net/` for Linux users, or `http://ftp.emini.dk/pub/php/win32/mcrypt/` for Windows users. It is pretty simple to do this; simply copy the library file to somewhere in your path (for neatness' sake, it's probably best to put it in the `ext` directory of your PHP installation) and enable the MCrypt module in the `php.ini` file.

Once you have got this installed, you can make use of the PHP CLI if you are using a recent version of PHP. The script I wrote is shown here:

```php
<?
$key = "Secret Key";
fwrite(STDOUT, "Please enter the encrypted details: \n");
$data = base64_decode(fgets(STDIN));
$decrypt = mcrypt_decrypt(MCRYPT_3DES, $key, $data, MCRYPT_MODE_CBC);
echo $decrypt;
?>
```

This was saved as `decrypt.php` and held in a secure folder on my personal machine. The file is used as follows from the command line:

```
C:\secure>php decrypt.php
Please enter the encrypted details:
j6Nwp+pzpSGKaijhyxMo7DgG1ZIReGkmDAJVgKJrhe8=
Order #52

Middle: 11111111
```

As you can see this has reversed the process of encryption and base64 encoding as expected, and spat out the original content of the email, which contains the all-important order number so that we can match the numbers correctly to the order. For more information on MCrypt, please see the documentation at `http://www.php.net/mcrypt`. Now you can proceed to use the details as normal. There are, however, several key things to note here:

1. The secret key used for encoding is contained within the script page. This means that this method is only as secure as the `cc.php` payment module file.

2. Base64 encoding was used to prevent the email client on your personal machine from flattening the encrypted string in its raw form. This is why it is necessary to apply base64 decoding to the input string before decryption takes place.

3. MCrypt has plenty of different encryption algorithms to offer, and you are not limited to the ones used in this script. You may also get warning from not using the optional final parameter—please look at the documentation for more information on this if it is a concern.

4. The method shown here can be improved upon by pulling the secret key value from a secure area of your site's file system, and using a proper key rather than a simple password.

5. Decrypting every credit card value may become tedious if you have a large number of orders.

6. You need to ensure that your live site has a version of PHP configured to make use of MCrypt.

7. You need to ensure that your personal machine has PHP and Mcrypt installed.

8. If you don't have access to MCrypt, look at what you *do* have. It isn't hard to redo this using GnuPG, for example. Make the most of the resources available to you, and remember to always test, test, and test. In this case, you would probably want to be able to catch any errors generated by MCrypt, and store the digits in a secure place instead of emailing them if there is a problem. The administrator would have to sort out the mess manually in this case.

Apart from being able to encrypt information sent within an email, this has also demonstrated how easy it is, with a bit of thought, to implement sufficient security to deter a fair amount of malicious intent. Remember that this is not foolproof just because you now have two files that contain the key used for the decryption—this means that both the server side and the administrator's machine are now in need of some good security to prevent intrusion.

With that done, let's turn our attention to the PsiGate payment module. The PsiGate module does not provide encryption facilities when sending its information to PsiGate, but it does target the secure PsiGate server so that the form information is transferred over SSL. Remember, you can also have customers supply their details directly to the PsiGate server by enabling the Remote option in the payment module's settings. This takes the back-end security responsibilities off your hands entirely.

Let's move on from the topic of security to look at a few community contributions that help to augment the facilities provide in the default distribution of osCommerce.

Low Stock Reports

By default, osCommerce comes with a few reports, which you can use to monitor your site. However, in all likelihood, at some stage you will find you want either better or different reports and report formats. Because of this, it is a good idea to install one of the report contributions, which is useful for maintaining good inventory control by alerting you to the fact that you might have certain products running out.

You know the drill by now, so make a backup of your site and then navigate to `http://www.oscommerce.com/community/contributions,1245/` in your browser to obtain a copy of the contribution. While you are there, you may as well browse around the other report contributions to see if there is anything that might also be of use. The low stock reports contribution is pretty simple to install! Follow these steps:

1. Copy the `admin/stats_low_stock.php` contribution file to `admin` on your site.

2. Copy the `admin/includes/languages/english/stats_low_stock.php` contribution file to the `admin/includes/languages/` directory on your site.

3. Add the following to `/admin/includes/languages/english.php`:
    `define('BOX_REPORTS_STOCK_LEVEL', 'Low Stock Report');`

4. Edit /admin/includes/boxes/reports.php by replacing:

```
'<a href="' . tep_href_link(FILENAME_STATS_CUSTOMERS, '', 'NONSSL') . '"
class="menuBoxContentLink">' . BOX_REPORTS_ORDERS_TOTAL . '</a>');
```

with the following:

```
'<a href="' . tep_href_link(FILENAME_STATS_CUSTOMERS, '', 'NONSSL') . '"
class="menuBoxContentLink">' . BOX_REPORTS_ORDERS_TOTAL . '</a><br>' .
'<a href="' . tep_href_link(FILENAME_STATS_LOW_STOCK, '', 'NONSSL') . '"
class="menuBoxContentLink">' . BOX_REPORTS_STOCK_LEVEL . '</a>');
```

5. Edit admin/includes/filenames.php by adding the line:

```
define('FILENAME_STATS_LOW_STOCK', 'stats_low_stock.php');
```

That's it, you are all done! Now if you go along to the Reports section in the admin tool, you will notice that you have a new Low Stock Report option, which, if clicked, will bring up the following page:

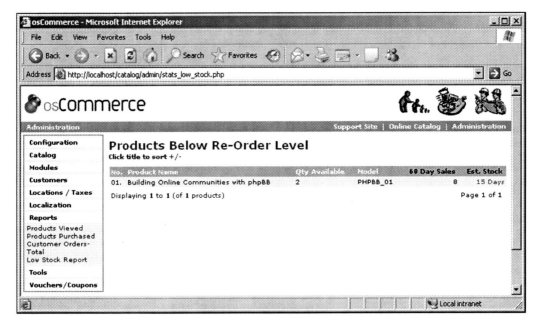

From this screenshot you can see that there is one product that has a stock less than the re-order level, which is set in the Configuration section of the admin tool on the Stock page. Two nice features of this report are that it shows the purchase history of the product for the last 60 days as well as an estimate for the amount of time it will take to deplete the remaining stock. In this case we have made eight sales in the last 60 days, and have about 15 days before we run out of this particular book totally.

Another thing to note is that if you have set up your stock control to allow checkout to go through even if a product is out of stock, then this report can show a negative value for the Qty Available column, meaning that you have these products on back order. Of course, if you have set the Allow Checkout setting to false, then it is not possible to get negative values here.

Working with Downloadable Products

Some of you may have had a nagging feeling that you shouldn't be allowing downloadable products to be downloaded until you actually have the payment in your account. You are obviously quite correct to be worried about this, because as it stands, the default behavior of osCommerce's download functionality will ruin you quite quickly.

Basically, what we want from the store is to only make a download available once a payment (be it PayPal, credit card, or whatever) has a certain order status. Now, what this means is that you need to look closely at all the payment methods you accept, and come up with an integrated policy that will allow you to make a call on whether something is downloadable or not with relative ease.

This probably sounds a bit confusing at the moment. It helps to think about it in terms of how a payment is processed. Recall that in Chapter 6 we used the PayPal IPN payment module to implement payments via PayPal. We had several statuses set for this type of payment, ranging from Denied, to Preparing [PayPal IPN], to Processing, and even Delivered. Recall too that while the status was set to Preparing [PayPal IPN], we had not actually received the funds in our account. It was only once we had accepted the funds that the status changed to Processing. It was then left to us to set the status to Delivered manually.

It should be clear to you that we don't want to make the download available when the status of the payment is Denied, or even when it is Preparing [PayPal IPN], because it is likely that the customer can download the product without ever forking out the cash. So in this case, we really want the download to be available only once we have reached the Processing or Delivered status.

Thankfully the Download Controller found at `http://www.oscommerce.com/community/contributions,135` can be of assistance here.

Installing the Download Controller

There are quite a lot of changes to make to your files, so back everything up now. One of the big problems with using this contribution is that it may well affect other contributions you already have installed. As a result, we have to make the modifications to altered files manually instead of replacing the files entirely.

The following instructions will get the controller working on your setup:

1. Add the following files:

    ```
    /catalog/includes/modules/shipping/freeshipper.php
    /catalog/includes/languages/english/modules/shipping/freeshipper.php
    /catalog/includes/modules/payment/freecharger.php
    /catalog/includes/languages/english/modules/payment/freecharger.php
    /catalog/images/icons/shipping_free_shipper.jpg
    /catalog/languages/english/images/buttons/button_download.gif
    /catalog/includes/functions/downloads_controller.php
    /catalog/includes/functions/webmakers_added_functions.php
    /catalog/includes/languages/webmakers_added_languages.php
    /catalog/includes/languages/english/downloads_controller.php
    /admin/includes/functions/webmakers_added_functions.php
    /admin/includes/languages/english/downloads_controller.php
    ```

2. Edit the following files:

    ```
    /catalog/includes/application_top.php:
    ```

Replace the line:

```
// Shopping cart actions
```
with:

```
// BOF: WebMakers.com Added: Functions Library
include(DIR_WS_FUNCTIONS . 'webmakers_added_functions.php');
// EOF: WebMakers.com Added: Functions Library
// Shopping cart actions
```

`/admin/includes/application_top.php:`
Add to the very bottom of the file just before the last ?>:

```
// BOF: WebMakers.com Added: Functions Library
include(DIR_WS_FUNCTIONS . 'webmakers_added_functions.php');
// EOF: WebMakers.com Added: Functions Library
```

`/catalog/includes/languages/english.php:`
Add to the very bottom of the file just before the last ?>:

```
// BOF: WebMakers.com Added: All Add-Ons
require(DIR_WS_LANGUAGES . 'webmakers_added_languages.php');
// EOF: WebMakers.com Added: All Add-Ons
```

`/admin/includes/languages/english.php:`
Add to the very bottom of the file just before the last ?>:

```
// BOF: WebMakers.com Added: All Add-Ons
require(DIR_WS_LANGUAGES . 'webmakers_added_languages.php');
// EOF: WebMakers.com Added: All Add-Ons
```

As well as these edits, you will also need to go through the following list of files and implement the changes between the contribution files and your store's files as shown.

3. Modify the following files by comparing the contribution file with the file in your store, and then incorporating the differences. (You may wish to use some sort of comparison software such as Beyond Compare, which you can find at `http://www.scootersoftware.com/`, for this.)

```
/catalog/includes/modules/downloads.php
/catalog/checkout_process.php
/catalog/checkout_shipping.php
/admin/orders.php
```

The actual changes aren't going to be listed in the text here because they will take up a fair amount of space and won't mean much to you anyway (you can always look at the files directly if you want to view the code for yourself). You should try to implement the changes, failing which you can view the actual modified files on the demo site.

I will give you the following handy hint though: you will probably get a MySQL error if you don't remove the following line from the contribution's code before you make use of the `checkout_process.php` file:

```
'comments' => $order->info['comments'],
```

This is because there is no `comments` column in the `orders` table. Apart from this, it is a case of going through each of the files in the previous list and carefully making changes or replacements as necessary.

Once that is all completed, it is time to get the contribution up and running so that you can start allowing downloadable products onto your site.

Working with the Download Controller

In order to make the **Download Controller** effective, you need to understand how it works. The most important thing to remember here is that a product will be made available depending on the value of its order status. The first thing to do is sort out your order status values by going to Orders Status in the Localization section of the administration tool and adding or removing statuses according to your needs.

Based on the needs of the demo site, the following settings were created by deleting all but Pending, which is the default, and adding the new statuses in order:

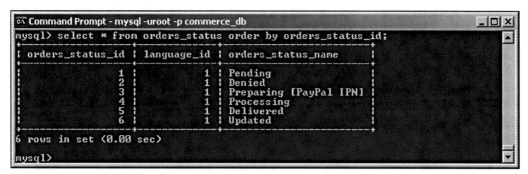

This screenshot shows you the command used to display the order statuses that have been saved on the system, using the MySQL client (you can always use phpMyAdmin or whatever else is available). Depending on what you need, you might decide to use different statuses, or simply different status IDs. As it stands on the demo site, we really want to allow downloads to be made available only for orders that have a status of 4 and above, because all others allow a customer to obtain the download without us first getting payment.

> Note that you will need to recheck the settings of your payment modules if you have just added these statuses to your system now. This is because the modules will probably still be picking up the old status ID values and giving you the wrong status!

In order to tell the download controller that it should only allow downloads based on these criteria, open up /catalog/includes/languages/english/downloads_controller.php and implement the following changes:

```
define('DOWNLOADS_AVAILABLE_STATUS','4');
```

As well as this, we need the Updated status to help the contribution perform a couple of actions needed after updating download settings on an order—the contribution also sends an email to the customer notifying him or her of this. To do this, simply go to /admin/includes/languages/english/downloads_controller.php and implement the following change:

```
define('ORDERS_STATUS_UPDATED_VALUE','6');
```

Obviously, if the order_status_id of your Updated status is not 6, then you would change this to reflect the value you have in your orders table. What this means is that if for some reason a customer had a problem with their download and you decided to allow him or her to try download it again, you could update the order status to Updated, and then set it back to whatever status is normal (say Delivered for argument's sake), and the customer would find that they are able to download the product again because the number of days and downloads that are available to the customer are refreshed.

The last thing we should do in order to make things as easy as possible on us is to remember that downloadable products do not weigh anything. If you have a product that is downloadable, then set its weight to 0 when you add it to your catalog. If a product has zero weight, then the shipping charges are not added to the product, which is exactly what you expect.

With everything set up, it is now time to test out the new download contribution.

Testing the Download Controller

The first thing you need to do is add a downloadable product to your database. So, if I wanted to sell an article for download, I would add it as per the instructions in Chapter 3 in the *Download* section, remembering to set the weight to zero. Once this has been done, we need to try to purchase this downloadable product using each and every one of the available payment methods.

For example, the following result was obtained directly after purchasing a downloadable item using PayPal:

This is perfect because the download is not available yet as we hoped. Note the highlighted message at the bottom of the screen, explaining that the download will not be available until we confirm the transaction. In the case of the demo site, the PayPal IPN module needs to set the status to Processing before the customer can download the product. This in turn only occurs once we have accepted the PayPal payment in PayPal itself.

Of course, you can set your downloads to deal with purchases however you see fit. There is quite a bit more to the download controller contribution that we don't have time to cover here since it has already provided us with what we initially needed it for. It is left to the reader to poke around and find out what else there is.

Creating Matching Buttons

Many of you will want to change the style of the buttons that are provided with osCommerce by default. If you do want to create your own set of buttons, then there is a good way and a bad way to go about it. The most important thing to do is simply create a button template, and once you have it, keep it safe and make sure it is never modified. If you need to create a new button, make a copy of this template, and write on it the new word that describes the button's function.

For example, some of you might like a plain old rectangle button, which looks nice and neat. If that's the case, then simply create a rectangle of the desired dimension, give it a border, and buttonize it. Whatever other effects you decide to add later on, you can. For example, the following button template was created and then included in the `includes\languages\english\images\buttons` folder:

Now, the only thing that you need to do is create a copy for each type of button you need, add the appropriate text in using whatever font, style, or color you like, and save it with the correct name so that osCommerce picks it up. The following example shows the button template being used for the Continue button on the login page, `button_continue.gif`, like so:

Remember too that you need to ensure that your buttons' file sizes are small—anything over 2kb, and it's probably too big. I'm sure you can come up with a better template yourself, and it's definitely worthwhile doing so in order to realize your site's own look and feel—it's also really fun! One thing to keep in mind is that you should keep your template in `.bmp` format or whatever is best for you, so that you can work with, and resize, the image properly. If you save the template as a GIF file, your options are limited, especially if you need to resize or create special effects.

If you want to be fancy, you might consider animating the buttons using Flash, but this isn't necessary, and sometimes ends up making the site look gaudy—it's really up to you!

Search Engine Optimization

One of the most common goals for today's e-commerce community is to appear high up on the big search engine rankings. As you should know, having a high ranking increases the chances of potential customers finding your site among the mass of other sites. So what is it that you can do to make your site rank as highly as possible without actually having to pay anyone to do it for you? Well, there is no straight answer to this, unfortunately, and many people will give you just as many different answers. However, there is a core set of things you can do that are known to help—they might vary in importance, but it is probably worth performing all of them. The following table highlights the most important optimizations or tasks, which you should consider performing:

Optimization	Explanation
Write web-enhanced copy	IMPORTANT: Think about how your target customers would find your store. What type of words would they use to find a shop like yours? Once you have come up with a list of key words and phrases, ensure that the writing on your site makes use of these phrases whenever possible.
	If you are using Google AdWords, then you can check the popularity of various search terms yourself—simply put them forward as potential target keywords and check on their stats, which Google provides before they are added.
	For example, if you are selling cellular phones, and you wanted to make the phrase cellular phone a term that you rank highly on, then instead of writing something like:
	This product can be used to call other people, you should write:
	This G1 super **cellular phone**, can call any other **cellular phone** from wherever you are.
	In other words, without destroying the readability of your website copy, fill it with relevant search terms. In this example, your copy went from not containing a single key phrase to containing two, without damaging the readability of the sentence in any way.
Use meaningful file names	While this is not as important as the first point, it certainly will help to have everything named meaningfully, because search engines do look at file names. Instead of naming a page `product_1.html`, you should name it something like `G1_cellularphone.html`. Don't go overboard on this because it is not too important.
Use meaningful anchor text	IMPORTANT: Search engines, in particular Google, place a large amount of emphasis on the anchor text used in links. As a result, make sure all your links have meaningful text associated with them. For example, you would rewrite the following sentence:
	Buy our new G1 Cellular Phone `<a href ="<yourlink>">here</a>`.
	to:
	Buy our new `<a href ="<yourlink>">Cellular Phone</a>` here.
	The reason for this is because the word here is not particularly meaningful to a search engine, even though humans can easily make the connection. For the sake of your rankings, simply move the link to the key phrase Cellular Phone to place more emphasis on it for the search engine.

Optimization	Explanation
Write meaningful metatags	As many people will tell you, metatags have become less and less important as time goes by. However, they are still useful, and you should at least go to the effort of filling them out properly. The two metatags that you should consider making use of are the keyword and description tags. For example, the following shows a possible tag for a cellular phone store:
	`<meta name="keywords" content="cellular phones cellphone phone mobile">`
	Metatags have been the subject of some abuse, and you should view the **W3C consortium's guidelines** for their usage: `http://www.w3.org`.
	The **Header Tags Controller** community contribution might be of interest to you here because it allows you to specify the title, keywords, and description on a per-page basis. You can find it at `http://www.oscommerce.com/community/contributions,207`.
Manage your links	IMPORTANT: A high level of importance is placed on the perceived popularity of a website. Search engines can judge the popularity of a website by looking at how many links there are to the site, and how popular the sites that link to it are themselves. For this reason, you should ensure that you link to and link from only sites that you feel are suitable partners.
	Effectively, you should search for as many relevant reciprocal link pages as possible, or actually speak to the relevant sites to determine whether you can provide mutual links. The more links you have from popular sites, the better your ranking will be. You can also try to get one-way links to your site—these are also rated highly by search engines.
Write meaningful `alt` tags for images	Search engines don't see pictures like humans do, so there is nothing you can do about images... or is there? Instead of naming your images `02_03.jpg`, you might consider giving them names like `G1_cellphone.jpg`. Don't stop there either. Instead of adding an image like this:
	`<img src="G1_cellphone.jpg">`
	write it like this:
	`<img src="G1_cellphone.jpg" alt="New super G1 cellular phone">`
Use meaningful URLs	osCommerce comes with several contributions that convert the standard osCommerce URLs into being more meaningful and search-engine friendly. If you decide to implement these, be sure to do so on your development machine, as the forums indicate a large number of problems associated with these contributions for highly modified sites.
	You might try `http://www.oscommerce.com/community/contributions,2823`.
Submit your site to search engines and online directories	Make sure your site is listed wherever possible. Most hosting packages provide an automated SE-submission facility, which will automatically forward your site to search engines for indexing. Otherwise, look for other SE web page submission tools, or search out your own lists and directories to become part of.
Read up on lists, forums, and online tutorials	There is a lot of helpful information out there. Make sure you do your own research and come up with an SEO policy that is right for you.

Of course, all of this work can be bypassed by getting a professional company to do this for you. However, if you are prepared to put in the time to develop your links and constantly upgrade your site, you will eventually recoup the benefits that accrue over time. However, don't expect everything to happen overnight!

Summary

Security is a great and very important challenge for any online retailer, and hopefully you will take it very seriously too. Remember that the more reliable online shopping or e-commerce is perceived to be by the general public, the more people will migrate to Internet-based commerce. Everyone who runs an e-commerce site has a responsibility to maintain strict security and protection standards in order to provide a safe and reliable environment for consumers everywhere. This chapter has put you well on the path to doing precisely this.

Since reporting facilities are such a commonplace requirement, we took the opportunity to look at how to implement more reporting into our store, as well as looking at how to make use of the community through a reporting contribution. We also did a bit of fun stuff, working on button templates, which will help to spruce up your site no end. This part of web development is always great fun for the creatively minded entrepreneur, but don't get too carried away and end up with a gimmicky store. Remember that you should only ever incorporate those things that actually add value in some quantifiable way.

The final part of this chapter looked at how to increase your store's profile on search engines through the use of search engine optimization. Ensuring that you have a high page ranking for your particular key terms is a very important factor in determining how much traffic your site generates. Think of the analogy like this: A high page ranking equates to having a high street store, where everyone walks past and peers in the window every day. Having a low page ranking is like owning a shop down a dark back alley where it is unlikely people will suddenly drop in.

By now you should pretty much be able to do whatever it is you wish in terms of adding and removing pictures, boxes, writing, buttons, banners, and so on. I'm sure you'll agree that owning and running an online business is one of the most multi-tasking, multi-discipline business opportunities that the modern world has to offer. The fundamentals of economics haven't changed though—work hard and look for the gaps, and you will do just fine.

Congratulations on finishing this book, and I wish you every success in your endeavors!

Troubleshooting

At some point in your career, you might experience problems with your code; no matter how diligently you try to work, errors do creep in. So common are errors (most often called **bugs**), in fact, that any big corporation nowadays has to implement comprehensive testing and debugging plans for months on end before it can consider new software to be fairly stable. Even then, as you have probably experienced, there are problems that slip under the radar and require patches or updates.

Since bugs are a part of life, it is better to learn how to deal with them properly than to hope to avoid them completely. This appendix will provide a few neat methods, as well as reiterate the best process for dealing with bugs. Remember, though, that if worst comes to absolute worst, and your site is beyond repair for one reason or another, then simply erase and fall back to your latest backup.

Types of Errors

Ensuring that your application is 'bug' or error free is a critical part of developing and building any software—and e-commerce websites are no different. There are different ways and means of isolating faults and correcting them, but before we look at those it is important to quickly acknowledge the different types of error that can make their unwelcome presence felt. Different types of errors also show in different ways and some are quite subtle and not easy to spot:

- **Syntax error**: These will prevent PHP from actually running your code, but on the plus side should be relatively easy to locate because of this. Of course, once your site is being used by the general public, you don't really want the internal errors in your system being reported to the screen, because this can often allow malicious users to glean information about your system.

- **Run-time error**: These are slightly worse than syntax errors because they are not quite as obvious, or easy to pin down. There are different ways in which a run-time error can occur, and many of these can only be caught by thorough testing on your site. For example, if you change file paths without the corresponding configuration changes, you end up with broken links, lost files, or disrupted database connections. While these errors won't show up when the PHP script is *parsed*, they will show up when it is executed.

- **Logic error**: These are quite sneaky in that they won't really show up at all. It is incumbent on you to decide whether your site is performing as it should. For example, accidentally typing a plus (+) sign instead of a minus (-) won't show up as either a run-time error or a syntax error, but will obviously affect the result of a calculation, which could have disastrous effects if it is part of your invoice calculator.

It is important that you are able to decide for yourself what type of error has occurred. Often, it takes a bit of experience to realize what an error message usually means because PHP can't always isolate the exact place an error has occurred. If you have already found yourself suffering from seemingly cryptic error messages, then read on to the *Debugging Code Yourself* section for help on a variety of issues.

An Effective Process for Dealing with Bugs

Whenever you encounter a bug that has a nontrivial or non-obvious solution, engage the following process to get it fixed:

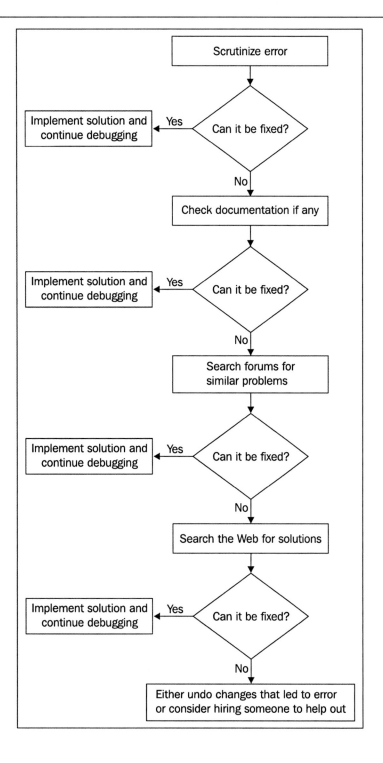

As you can see, the outlined process begins by trying to solve the problem yourself, and in the event that you can't, it incrementally increases the scope of the search for solutions. Ideally, however, you don't want to have to upgrade the problem to hours of searching on the Internet if at all possible. You simply want to be able to deal with the problem yourself and move on. In order to be able to do this with any sort of confidence, you need two things:

- Experience
- A toolkit for solving problems

Unfortunately, you can't gain experience from a book, so the next section will focus on giving you the tools to complete the job—how much experience you gain is really up to you. Once you have a few tricks of the trade under your belt, you will find that solving problems becomes, more often than not, a satisfying occupation. Remember, that every time you attempt to solve a problem in your code, you are learning more about the software, which will in turn help you the next time round.

Debugging Code Yourself

Before we continue, I should mention that we will demonstrate some fairly complex debugging using the example code given in the professional version of the book. Please bear in mind that it is not important for you to have this code in order to follow along—the important thing is you appreciate the *manner in which the error was detected and corrected*.

Let's begin with a couple of the easier-to-solve syntax problems. PHP will kick up a variety of different errors depending on where and how the syntax problem has caused an error in the script. For example, if you added a line to your code in order to perform a task (perhaps you added an extra echo statement), but get the following screen when you run the script:

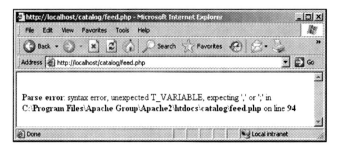

Looking at this error, you can see that on line 94 of the feed.php script (don't worry if you don't have this particular page yourself—it is a custom page used for this demo), the PHP interpreter expects to find a , or ;, but instead it has come across something called a T_VARIABLE. A T_VARIABLE is simply PHP's name for a variable defined in your script. So the English translation of this error is:

I have come across one of your variables instead of what I expected, namely a comma or semi-colon, on line 94 of the feed.php script in the c:\Program Files\Apache Group\Apache2\htdocs\catalog directory.

If we take a look at that spot in the code, we see the following:

```
} else{
    echo "<font face='Verdana' size='2'>Previous</font>";
}

echo "</td><td align=center width='30%'>"
$i=0;
$1=1;
for($i=0;$i < $numrows;$i=$i+$limit){
```

Can you see the error? We simply forgot to insert a semi-colon to finish off the echo statement so PHP didn't realize the line had ended and ended up coming across $i unexpectedly. Adding one fixes the problem, and the script runs as normal. So far so good, but what about other types of syntax error? What can we expect to get from PHP if, for example, we miss out a brace two lines above the echo statement? Reasonably, you could assume that it should report that there is a missing brace on line 92 (since the closing brace is two lines above the echo statement from the previous example), couldn't you?

Well, removing the closing brace from the else statement in the previous code snippet gives the following error message:

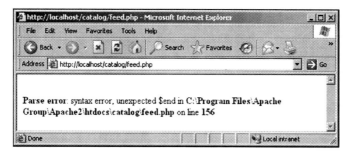

Oh dear, this is not very helpful; line 156 is the very last line of the script, and we happen to know already that it is line 92 which is causing the problem. How have things gone wrong, and what is PHP trying to tell us? The problem here lies in the fact that PHP doesn't really know what your program does, it simply takes it for granted you know what you are doing. So when you open a brace, it will treat everything that follows as part of that code block until it finds a matching closing brace—even if this is not what you intended. In our case, there is no matching closing brace, so PHP is telling us:

> I got to the end of the file, but that is unexpected because you haven't finished your script properly.

This is where having a good PHP editor comes in. If you are using something like the Zend development environment, then the script editor is PHP-aware and can often help pinpoint problems like this because it automatically indents code so that it is a lot easier to see problems like this by simply looking at the file. Which do you think is easier to understand, this:

```
feed.php - Notepad                                                    _ □ X
File  Edit  Format  View  Help
<td class="pageHeading" align="right"><?php echo tep_image(DIR_WS_IMAGES . 'table_background_specials.gif',
HEADING_TITLE, HEADING_IMAGE_WIDTH, HEADING_IMAGE_HEIGHT); ?></td>□        </tr>□
</table></td>□      </tr>□      <tr>□        <td><?php echo tep_draw_separator('pixel_trans.gif', '100%', '10');
?></td>□      </tr>□      <tr>□        <td><table border="0" width="100%" cellspacing="0" cellpadding="2">□
<tr>□        <td class="main"><?php □                    □if(!isset($_GET['start']))
{    □$start = 0;□}else {□$start = $_GET['start'];□}□□$initval = ($start - 0);  □$limit = 10;          □$now = $initval +
$limit;  □$back = $initval - $limit;  □$next = $initval + $limit;  □□$find_rows = tep_db_query("select count(*) from
feed;");□$numrows=mysql_result($find_rows, 0);□□$gather_feed_query = tep_db_query("select link, title,
description, added from feed limit $initval, $limit;");□□while($query_data = mysql_fetch_array($gather_feed_query)){□
$link = html_entity_decode($query_data['link']);□  $title = html_entity_decode($query_data['title']);□  $description =
html_entity_decode($query_data['description']);□  $date = $query_data['added'];□  echo "<a class='feed' href=\"$link\"
target=\"_blank\" title=\"\">$title </a><a align=\"right\">$date</a>";□  echo "<br><a href=\"$link\" target=\"_blank\"
title=\"\">$description </a><br>";□}                                 □echo "<table align = 'center'
width=50%'><tr><td align='left' width='30%'>";□□if($back >=0) {  □  echo "<a href='" .
tep_href_link(FILENAME_FEED) . '&start=' . $back ."'><font face='Verdana' size='2'>Previous</font></a>";  □} else{□
echo "<font face='Verdana' size='2'>Previous</font>";□□□echo "</td><td align=center width='30%'>";□$i=0;□
$l=1;  □for($i=0;$i < $numrows;$i=$i+$limit){□  if($i <> $initval){□    echo " <a href='" .
```

Or this:

```
feed.php                                                              _ □ X
[toolbar icons]
|----+----1----+----2----+----3----+----4----+----5----+----6----+----7----+----8----+----|
       align=\"right\">$date</a>";
 82     echo "<br><a href=\"$link\" target=\"_blank\" title=\"\">$description </a><br>";
 83  }
 84
 85  echo "<table align = 'center' width='50%'><tr><td  align='left' width='30%'>";
 86
 87  if($back >=0) {
 88     echo "<a href='" . tep_href_link(FILENAME_FEED) . '&start=' . $back ."'><font
        face='Verdana' size='2'>Previous</font></a>";
 89  } else{
 90     echo "<font face='Verdana' size='2'>Previous</font>";
 91
 92
 93  echo "</td><td align=center width='30%'>";
▶94  $i=0;
 95  $l=1;
 96  for($i=0;$i < $numrows;$i=$i+$limit){
 97    if($i <> $initval){
 98       echo " <a href='" . tep_href_link(FILENAME_FEED) . '&start=' . $i . "'><font
          face='Verdana' size='2'>" . $i . "</font></a> ";
 99    } else { echo " <font face='Verdana' size='2' color='red'>$l</font> ";}
100       $l=$l+1;
```

As you can see, a proper editor makes life a lot easier because from this screenshot, we can see that there should be a brace inserted after the fourth visible echo statement, but before the fifth. How? Well, look at the code indenting, if the fifth echo statement was part of the else block, it would also be indented. Of course, this is slightly contrived, but you get the picture—make sure you have a reasonable code editor before you attempt any serious debugging.

What about slightly more tricky problems, such as errors in the code's logic? Perhaps you have noticed that while no errors are being thrown up by PHP, your web page doesn't behave as you expect. Problems like this require a slightly more sophisticated approach. Let's say, for example, that when viewing the feed.php page in the browser, you notice that the navigation at the bottom of the page is not working properly—an example is shown here:

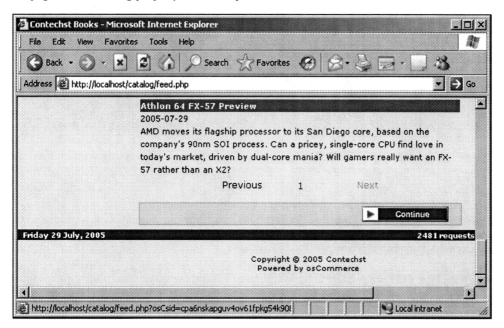

The above screenshot also highlights why it is so important to test everything thoroughly. Can you spot the problem? Well, the navigation links at the bottom of the feed page show that there is only one page, yet as you can clearly see, the Next button can still be activated, implying that there are more than ten items in the feed (the feed.php script is set to allow for ten results per page). This is a bit of a problem: either there are only ten items in the feed, in which case the Next button should not be active, or there are more than ten items in the feed, in which case there should be more than one page of feed items.

So what do we do in this case?—there are no fatal errors or warnings to guide us, so we are on our own. Well, luckily for us, a large part of the analysis of the problem has been done for us already, because we know how this part of the application should behave. In other words, the problem is simple to understand—this doesn't necessarily mean it has a simple solution, but knowing what we want to achieve is an important step to rectifying any problem.

Furthermore, we have already advanced two plausible explanations for the problem. Either the Next button is not behaving properly or the pagination display is not working correctly. What's the next step? Do we jump in and try to fix the code? Not yet; there is something else we can do to further clarify the problem. Since we have access to the database, let's find out how many records there actually are—this will tell us whether we should have more pages than we do.

A quick visit to the MySQL command line tells us the following:

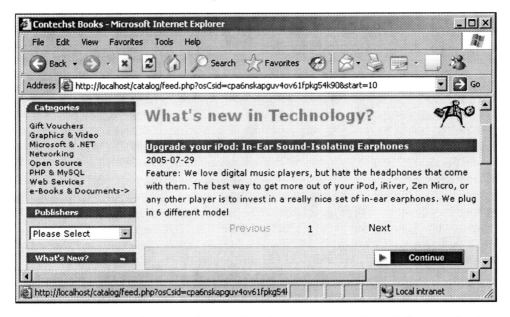

We have eleven items in the feed table, which means that the pagination display is definitely not working correctly. Do we go fix it yet? Not yet; just because the pagination display is not working, doesn't automatically imply that the Next and Previous links are. Let's test those quickly before we do anything. With 11 rows in the database, we expect the first page to have an inactive Previous link and an active Next link. If we click the Next link, the following page should have an active Previous link, an inactive Next link, and only one item. Trying this all out confirms that under these circumstances, the links are working correctly:

Before we go any further, there are a few considerations to point out. First of all, the pagination and links may work for the given number of items in the database. Just because they do, you shouldn't assume that they work for any number of items. Any page should be tested with a wide variety of item quantities to ensure they work correctly. Second, if the Previous and Next links didn't work, then there was nothing you could assume about the nature of the problem, because either there is a separate source of error for the pagination and the links, or there is a common link causing the errors in both—you can't tell with the information you have.

> When debugging, try to keep your mind completely free of assumptions about the nature of the error.

OK, so we can consider the problem to be fairly well analyzed now. We understand how the code is supposed to work, and we have gathered information to help us eliminate certain possibilities as well as confirm certain suspicions. Having done all this, we should still try to keep a clear view of things, because often problems can have very unexpected or subtle causes, which are hard to find if you act predominantly on assumption. With the analysis done, we now need to begin examining the code in order to understand the nature of the problem.

This is where certain tricks come into play. Two of the most common questions a programmer needs answered are:

- What values are being held in variables at a given point of program execution?
- How is the program being executed?

Now, at this point it is probably worth mentioning that you can obtain something called an **Integrated Development Environment (IDE)** for developing and debugging code. Zend, the people who make PHP, have a development studio available, and you can look over their products at http://www.zend.com/store/products/zend-studio/. This comes with a suite of facilities to help you sort out problems like this. For example, you can expect:

- A Code analyzer
- Code completion
- Syntax highlighting
- A Project manager
- A Code editor
- A Graphical debugger
- Wizards

All of these work together to help you create better code, and debug and analyze any code that you already have. If, however, you don't feel the need to fork out cash to work on your projects, then you might want to consider something like the freely available Dev-PHP, found at http://devphp.sourceforge.net/. However, you can do a fairly useful job of discovering variable content and program execution all by yourself by employing the following methods:

- echo variable contents to the screen
- echo program execution markers to the screen

Let's take a look at how this can help us to solve the feed page problem.

Knowing that we are most likely looking at a pagination display problem alone, let's focus our efforts on seeing what is happening under the hood. Hopefully, this will reveal where the flaw is occurring so that we can modify it and solve the problem. First thing's first, let's find the relevant section of code:

```
$i=0;
$l=1;
for($i=0;$i < $numrows;$i=$numrows+$limit){
   if($i <> $start){
      echo " <a href='" . tep_href_link(FILENAME_FEED) . '&start=' . $i .
"'><font face='Verdana' size='2'>" . $l . "</font></a> ";
   } else { echo " <font face='Verdana' size='2' color='red'>$l</font> ";}
      $l=$l+1;
}
```

This snippet is responsible for outputting the pages. The first thing we notice is that it makes use of the $numrows variable, which is declared elsewhere. Let's go look for that declaration, so we understand what type of value it should contain. Looking up the page we find:

```
$find_rows = tep_db_query("select count(*) from feed;");
$numrows=mysql_result($find_rows, 0);
```

Ah ha! Notice that $numrows should contain the number of records in the database. Recall that earlier we used the same SQL query to determine this value. We are also making use of the $limit and $start variables, which we need to find as well. Searching earlier in the code, we find:

```
if(!isset($_GET['start'])) {
$start = 0;
}else {
$start = $_GET['start'];
}

$limit = 10;
```

From this we can see that the $start variable contains the value of $i, which is the iterator variable for the for loop, and $limit is simply the number of items to show per page. Since we are not getting the right number of pages printed out to the screen, let's take a look at how the for loop is working in more detail. In order to do this, we want to track the values of the variables being used as well as the program execution. Accordingly, we can use a debugging modification like this:

```
$i=0;
$l=1;
for($i=0;$i < $numrows;$i=$numrows+$limit){
   echo "We are in the for loop here: <br>";
   echo '$i = ' . $i . "<br>";
   echo '$l = ' . $l . "<br>";
   echo '$numrows = ' . $numrows . "<br>";
   echo '$limit = ' . $limit . "<br>";
   if($i <> $start){
      echo "  We are in the if statement here: <br>";
      echo '  $i = ' . $i . "<br>";
      echo '  $l = ' . $l . "<br>";
      echo '  $numrows = ' . $numrows . "<br>";
      echo '  $start = ' . $start . "<br>";

      echo " <a href='" . tep_href_link(FILENAME_FEED) . '&start=' . $i .
"'><font face='Verdana' size='2'>" . $l . "</font></a> ";
   } else { echo " <font face='Verdana' size='2' color='red'>$l</font> ";
      echo "    We are in the else block: <br>";
```

```
        echo '     $i = ' . $i . "<br>";
        echo '     $l = ' . $l . "<br>";
        echo '     $numrows = ' . $numrows . "<br>";

        $l=$l+1;
    }
}
```

Generally, you don't need to be quite as verbose as the above statements. If you have a fairly good idea of what is going on, you simply need to echo one or two values to the screen to find out what is happening. Looking at the results of the above modifications, we see that for the first page our results are:

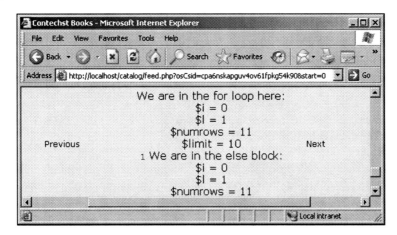

Straightaway you should get the nagging suspicion that something is wrong, because we are only going through the loop once before finishing. What's worse, our if condition never evaluates to true before the for loop ends its single iteration. The values we have outputted all seem to be in order for what we would expect for the first iteration of the for loop, so immediately we should suspect that something is wrong with the actual for loop conditions. Let's take a closer look at them here:

```
for($i=0;$i < $numrows;$i=$numrows+$limit){
```

Agh! What a silly mistake! Looking at the for loop condition from a structural point of view, we have asked it to do the following:

1. Begin the loop with $i equal to zero.
2. Test if $i is less than $numrows.
3. If it is, then execute the code block.
4. Evaluate the final expression $i = $numrows + $limit.
5. Repeat steps 2 to 4.

From the output of our echo statements, shown in the previous figure, we can see that initially:

```
$numrows = 11
$limit = 10
```

So, when step 4 is evaluated, $i is assigned the value 21. Moving to step 5 redirects us to step 2, which asks us to test that $i (21) is less than $numrows (11), which it quite clearly isn't, so the for loop breaks out, and we move on without performing any more actions. To be honest, this example is slightly contrived because an experienced programmer would have immediately noticed that $numrows + $limit > $numrows because $limit > 0.

For the purposes of learning how to monitor program execution, this is perfect because we noticed an unexpected result in that the for loop was only executing *once*. So, we need to modify the for loop so that it executes the correct number of times. In order to do this, we need to think carefully about what it is we want the loop to achieve. Effectively, we need it to take the number of items there are in the database, and divide by the record limit per page in order to decide how many pages to create. Then for each page, it needs to create a numbered link to those results, except for the current page, which is not a link.

Modifying the third condition of the for loop to the following:

```
for($i=0;$i < $numrows;$i=$i+$limit){
```

fixes the problem because whatever the value of $numrows, the for loop will iterate the correct number of times because we are increasing the value of $i by $limit each time. Trying the debugged code again gives the following results:

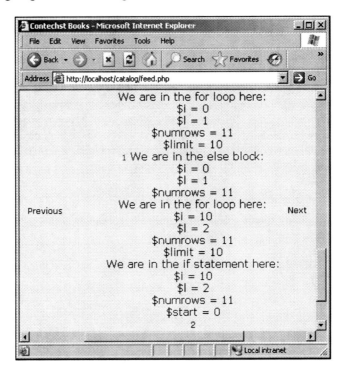

Looking closely at this output, you can see that there is now a 2 outputted at the bottom of the screen. This is as we would expect, because there are two pages required for eleven feed items. The for loop finishes after the first if statement (not counting the initial execution of the else block) because after that $i has a value of 20.

Finally, you can see that the second time we enter the for loop, $i has a value of 10. Because of this, we enter the if statement because $i (10) is not equal to $start (0) because we are on the first page. This means we output a link to the second page and set the value of $start to 10 by appending it to the URL of the link.

Summary

While there is really no substitute for experience, you cannot really join the fray without some tools to help you on your way. This appendix has shown you how to deal with a few of the more common and simpler errors, which occur reasonably often. Following this, a good process for dealing with more complex problems was outlined by way of example using the feed page code, which was created in the professional version of this book.

From this you have learned to gather information and analyze a problem before diving into the code. Once you have established what you expect the code to do (make sure you understand enough to have the correct expectations), you can go about determining possible causes. As well as this, you learned a few tricks for helping illuminate the program's execution so that you provide yourself with important debugging information.

Remember that many development environments provide all sorts of features that can make your life easier—if you find that you don't have time to invest in doing things manually, then using one of the PHP IDEs on the market is certainly a worthwhile alternative.

Index

N

R

reports
    low stock reports, 159

S

search engine optimization, 166
security. *See* **osCommerce security**
sessions, administration, 52
shipping
    charging per item, 138
    flat rate module, 136
    modules, 136
    per item module, 138
    shipping policy, 142
    shipping table, 138
    table rate module, 138
    UPS, 139
    zone rates module, 142
shipping details, administration, 43
shipping table, 138
specials, 70

SSL

SSL
    .htaccess file, changes, 150
    implementing, 150-152
stocks, administration, 46
store, administration, 36

T

table rate, shipping module, 138
tax
    classes, 116
    rates, 116, 117
    zones, 114
troubleshooting, 29, 169

U

United Parcel Service. shipping option, 139
    See also **shipping**

Z

zone rate, shipping module, 142

Thank you for buying Building Online Stores with osCommerce: Beginner Edition

Packt Open Source Project Royalties

When we sell a book written on an Open Source project, we pay a royalty directly to that project. Therefore by purchasing *Building Online Stores with osCommerce: Beginner Edition* Packt will have given some of the money received to the osCommerce project.

In the long term, we see ourselves and you—customers and readers of our books—as part of the Open Source ecosystem, providing sustainable revenue for the projects we publish on. Our aim at Packt is to establish publishing royalties as an essential part of the service and support a business model that sustains Open Source.

If you're working with an Open Source project that you would like us to publish on, and subsequently pay royalties to, please get in touch with us.

Writing for Packt

We welcome all inquiries from people who are interested in authoring. Book proposals should be sent to authors@packtpub.com. If your book idea is still at an early stage and you would like to discuss it first before writing a formal book proposal, contact us; one of our commissioning editors will get in touch with you.

We're not just looking for published authors; if you have strong technical skills but no writing experience, our experienced editors can help you develop a writing career, or simply get some additional reward for your expertise.

About Packt Publishing

Packt, pronounced 'packed', published its first book "*Mastering phpMyAdmin for Effective MySQL Management*" in April 2004 and subsequently continued to specialize in publishing highly focused books on specific technologies and solutions.

Our books and publications share the experiences of your fellow IT professionals in adapting and customizing today's systems, applications, and frameworks. Our solution-based books give you the knowledge and power to customize the software and technologies you're using to get the job done. Packt books are more specific and less general than the IT books you have seen in the past. Our unique business model allows us to bring you more focused information, giving you more of what you need to know, and less of what you don't.

Packt is a modern, yet unique publishing company, which focuses on producing quality, cutting-edge books for communities of developers, administrators, and newbies alike. For more information, please visit our website: www.PacktPub.com.

Printed in the United States
108955LV00002B/46/A